John 3:16

Mine

Or

His

A true story of Forgiveness and Purpose

Robert (Bob) Stavenger

Acknowledgments

N.I.V. Bible for all scripture quotes

Amy Dees for your help with editing the book

John Conrad for writing the forward

Lonna for your story

Pastor Rhys Stenner for your mention, encouragement and prayer

Hugh Kirby for your mention and prayer

My children Sheila, Julia, CJ, and Jennifer for your encouragement
(I love you)

My siblings Paul, Donna and Kathy

New Hope Baptist Church for helping me grow as a Christian

City of Fayetteville Police Department for your mention

FOREWARD

We all love a good story, and all the better if we know it is a true one! We even have sayings like "Truth is stranger than fiction" and "You can't make this stuff up!" to emphasize the joy of a good narrative. In "Mine or His" Bob Stavenger shares the fascinating story of his search for purpose, and how he found and gave the freedom of forgiveness in the process.

Just as we all love a good story, we all have a life story that is shaped and fashioned (some would say hammered & hewn) by the struggles and blessings of life. What I like about Bob's story, is how often as I read I could identify with him, and especially with the pursuing love of God that permeates this book.

Bob's book is honest & earthly. It is heartwarming and humorous, interesting and inspiring. There are Scripture references throughout that serve as road signs on Bob's journey, but I also found them very helpful for my own path. The transparency of Bob's testimony, including mistakes and struggles, give his writing and endearing humility. Some of my favorite parts include his police work as "Officer Bob" as well as Bob's participation in the New Hope Church Choir, which is how I have known him for the last 20 years. During that time, I have seen Bob grow in his faith and service. A man who hid out on the back row of the bass section, has become a bold worshiper and witness for Jesus Christ. I see pictures in my mind's eye of Bob leading men in prayer, arms locked in a circle, calling on the Holy Spirit to move. Bob singing (and swaying) in a Gospel Choir on Mission in Wales, and Bob raising a lantern, dressed in Biblical Costume, to sing and celebrate the Savior's birth. I see him with hands lifted, tears running, singing "Total Praise".

But what Bob does best is tell a story. This is his story, but Bob would be quick to say it is His (God's) story. And what a glorious story it is.

"Looking unto Jesus the Author and Finisher of our Faith..." Heb. 12:2

John Conrad
Associate Pastor
NHBC
Music & Missions

Introduction

Looking for my purpose!

Ecclesiastes 3:1 To every thing there is a season, and a time to every purpose under the heavens.

Okay so…...Don't you love it when the first sentence of a book starts with Okay so…..anyway, I was sitting with some friends one day and we were sharing some stories of our experiences in law enforcement. Most of my friends are police officers, firefighters and federal employees. Some are engineers who work for Delta Airlines and elevator companies. A friend suggested we write a book. Nobody else liked the idea of writing a book but I thought about his suggestion and I decided to put pen to paper and share some of my thoughts. As I was writing I felt God saying "I don't want you to write this book". I played this off as my own personal doubts about writing a book. I felt the same nudge several times when I began to write. I finally said "Okay what would you like me to write about"? As clear as the nose is on my face was, and that's pretty clear, because some would say my nose is quite large, I heard "I want you to write about your personal testimony". My testimony? WOW! Where do I start? I said Okay I think I can do that. I am new to this and I was not even sure what to do. How do I do this? Where to begin? When I first thought about writing this book I wasn't sure where the starting point in my life was going to be. I know I wanted God to lead this endeavor for sure. God gave me this opportunity and I want to Honor and Glorify Him first and foremost. I wanted this to be about how my life changed, how I developed a personal relationship with Jesus Christ. Most Christians I know have been a Christian most of their life. I however became a Christian when I was 32 years old, January 21, 1990 to be exact. I have plenty of life experiences to share and my thoughts were to write my testimony and then leave it there. I was wondering would people even want to read about my struggles and would they be interesting enough to read. But then I thought It would leave people wondering about my life prior to knowing my Savior. Do people even want to know about me before I met our Lord and Savior. This could be embarrassing to say the least. I spoke to a few friends and they gave me their thoughts about how I should do this. Ironically I have always said my life was not an open book. Well now it is, sort of, and I'm writing it. I don't want to put all of my life in words, only a few of the more important things which caused me to wander a bit. I don't want this to be a pity or a bashing party, I am way beyond that, I want to tell a story about how I was feeling and how things were back then, which will eventually make sense (I hope), my purpose found, and in the end…...all is forgiven!

Matthew 6:14-15 For if you forgive other people when they sin against you, your heavenly father will also forgive you. But if you do not forgive others their sins, your father will not forgive your sins.

So here goes everything!

DEDICATION

To my Mom and Dad. Thanks for putting up with my behavior growing up. For believing in me when I didn't. For forgiving me for all of my transgressions. For loving me through all of this, but especially for not giving up on me in Trenton.

To my wife Mary. You have been with me through it all, never leaving my side and always believing in me. Giving me our first parking lot kiss. Holding me when I needed it even when I didn't think I did. For living through the life of a policeman's wife. You deserve a medal.

I LOVE YOU ALL

My Prayer

May our Lord and Savior get all of the Praise,
Honor and Glory which will hopefully come out
of these words. I pray for whoever reads this
and does not know the Lord as their personal
Savior these words will tell them there is hope,
and you will find your purpose and trust in
Him. This is not my promise but Gods. John
3:16 says; For God so loved the world that He
gave His one and only Son, that whoever
believes in Him shall not perish but have
eternal life. If He can save me I know He can
save you too.

Amen

How it all began!

I was born in Trenton New Jersey. Our family had gone there to visit my moms sister Dorothy, everyone call her Dot. Dad was in the Air Force and was stationed at Dover AFB in Dover Delaware. A short weekend trip turned into a long month of worry. My mother's due date was in July but I had different plans. On May 4, 1957 I came into the world, two months early and I was extremely small. I weighed 4lbs 4ozs and was so tiny my dad said I could fit in a small shoe box. Mom said the days were long and that minutes seemed like hours. My weight had dropped to 3lbs 9ozs and I was not doing well at all. Mom said the doctors gave me about a 20% chance of survival. During my first week of life here on earth my weight fluctuated, my breathing was labored and my heart actually stopped 4 times. The doctors and nurses were with me around the clock wondering each day and asking themselves, would he make it through the night? Eventually I began to gain weight an ounce here and an ounce there. My mom said every ounce gained was a celebration. My breathing improved and at 5lbs and 8oz I finally went home. The doctors called me a medical miracle. It took a month.

Colossians 1:16 For in Him all things were created; things in heaven and on earth, visible and invisible, whether thrones or powers or rulers or authorities; all things have been created through Him and for Him.

The early years

My life was a hectic one from the start. Dad was in the Air Force and stationed in Delaware when he received orders to go to Okinawa Japan. We packed up the house and moved to Greenville New Hampshire and stayed with my grandparents (Meme' and Pepe') for a little while. We were waiting for dad to get housing so we could later go and join him. I really missed him a lot. My grandparents house had a phone that was located next to the front door at the bottom of the stairs. When dad would call, usually it would be very late in the evening, we would all get a brief chance to say hello. It was cool! I would anxiously wait for his next call so I could talk to him. I don't remember my Pepe' much I was very young when he died but I do remember he loved to watch the Red Socks play on TV, and our trips to the cider mill to get apple cider. He would always take a bottle and put it in his workshop. We were told to not touch "Pepe's cider". Hmm I wonder why! We would sit at the kitchen table and I remember when he would eat very sharp aged white cheddar cheese and granny smith apples. He used his pocketknife to cut the apples into slices. He would give us a taste every now and then. I didn't care for the cheese back then but I love it now. What a great memory with him. My memory of my Meme' was a little bit better because she lived with us for a while after my dad retired from the Air Force. Living in Greenville was pretty cool. My Meme' would have lunch for us when we would come home from school. The school house was at the top of the hill next to my grandmothers house and we would walk down the hill to eat lunch with her. She would have either a banana sandwich or a Fluff-a-Nutter sandwich waiting for us. That was peanut butter and marshmallow fluff. I still have them from time to time. She would also have for us a pint size glass bottle of milk and some chips. One of my fondest memories was when Pepe' would let us use his workshop to make wooden boats. He would give us some scrap wood, a saw and some nails and we would make boats. He would give us some string and we would tie it to the boats and we would walk to the bridge next to his house, lower the boats into the river and float them around for awhile. I don't think my mom liked it too much because she always thought we would fall in the river. It was a lot fun and of course, we didn't fall in the river. After about 9 months or so we left New Hampshire, my mom and four kids in tow, and off to Okinawa we go via San Francisco, Hawaii, Wake Island and then Okinawa yippee! I have no idea how my mom did it but she did. She is a strong and independent woman with a lot of patience. When we got off the plane in Okinawa I saw my dad walking towards us on the tarmac and I took off running to meet him. I was so glad to see him. Okinawa was a great place, tropical weather and beaches, lots of fireworks during the Japanese holidays. Fun for kids for sure. I remember meeting an actor named Fess Parker. He played Daniel Boone on a TV show back in the 60's. He did a play at my school. Block parties were big back then and were usually held in the parking lot of the condos where we lived. There would be a live band that would play. I got my inspiration to play the guitar from those parties. My parents gave me a toy guitar for Christmas one year and I really like playing it. It wasn't a good guitar but none the less I play the fool out of it. I wanted a better one and so I saved my allowance and dad took me to a pawn shop where I bought a Kawai acoustic guitar. It cost me five dollars. That was a lot of money for a seven-year-old kid back then. I played it all the time. My youngest sister Kathy was about 3 or 4 years old and was playing in our neighbors back yard across the parking lot. One of the boys she was playing with came running over banging on the door yelling Kathy had fallen into the sewer drain and could not get out. My mom, my brother Paul and I ran over to see what had happen. At first we thought that she had fallen into what was called a benjo ditch which was an oriental sewer drain, when we got there we found she had fallen into a manhole that was uncovered and was actually drowning in, what I will say was muck. I ran to get help and found a Japanese man who worked at the restaurant next to our building. He was very tall which was unusual for the Japanese and we ran back to where Kathy was. Paul had tried to get her out with a rope and she would not grab it. The Japanese guy reached down into the hole and was able to grab her and pull her out. Kathy and my parents spent the rest of the day at the hospital. Later the local news got wind of the incident and did an article in the paper about it. My brother and the Japanese guy were heralded as hero's and got their pictures in the paper. I always wondered why I was not recognized. I was the one who got the man who saved my sisters life. I believe my parents now saw Paul as the hero of the family and he could do no wrong. Maybe it was because he tried to save her with the rope. That was probably it.

Where is my purpose?.......you can't see it!

After Okinawa dad got orders to Ellsworth AFB in Rapid City South Dakota. We left Okinawa on Christmas Day and arrived in San Francisco on Christmas Day about 12 hours earlier. We tried to have two Christmas's but I guess mom and dad were smarter than we were. Then the adventure started. We drove a 1959 Chevrolet station wagon, from San Francisco to Rapid City. Dad had painted it battleship gray with some old paint they were throwing away at work. This was in 1965 so the car was still in good shape and of course it was a Chevrolet so we could drive it to the moon and back. Dad was a big GM guy, nothing but Chevrolet's and Buick's. Being in South Dakota was fun most of the time. We lived at an old Nike missile site at the housing unit there. We would sometimes go and climb the fence and run around the old missile concrete covers that covered the missile silos. Every time a helicopter would fly over we would hide so we didn't get in trouble for being there. There wasn't any missiles there so I don't think it really mattered much. We also played in the farmers fields. There were frog ponds all over the place and we all had BB guns and we would try and shoot the frogs. They were a lot faster than we were. We also played broom stick army. We would use a broom stick for a gun and we would go out and play army and of course being Air Force brats we would have an airport set up and land our model planes on the runway. It was an elaborate set up, at least I thought so. There were times however when it was rough for me. I kept getting bronchitis and had to be in quarantine (my bedroom) with a hot air vaporizer and Vick's vapor rub. It worked great as long as I stayed in my room, but as soon as I left my room I would start coughing again and I would have to go back to my dungeon. The snowstorms there were sometimes extreme. One year we were stranded for a week because the snow was so deep not even the plows could get to us. As a kid it was great because there was NO SCHOOL! We did a lot of camping in South Dakota. Mainly in the Black Hills and mostly at Sheraton Lake.. We had a pop-up camper. My brother Paul and I would sleep in a tent and my sisters, Donna and Kathy, would sleep in the pop up with mom and dad. We did a lot of fishing, boating and hanging out with the family. I remember going to Mt. Rushmore several times. I never got sick of seeing those guys on the side of that mountain. Dad worked with a guy named Skip. He and his wife Diane would come with us sometimes. Diane was really cool and funny. We were roasting marshmallows one time and Diane put almost an entire bag of them in her mouth. It was supper funny and we laughed a lot, she was great. I was not very fond of Skip though. There was something about him I did not care for. He was always loud, and he would yell and laugh at me a lot. One day I was at my favorite fishing spot and Skip came over to where I was. He pushed me out of my chair and took my spot. I told him he was in my fishing spot and I asked him to move. As a seven-year-old would do I tried to push him out of the chair, he turned and slapped me pretty hard across my face. I got so mad I called him a bad name. I won't repeat it here. I was crying, and he was laughing, and he would not get up from my spot. I ran to my dad and told him what had happened and what I had said. Instead of him speaking with Skip, I got grounded for saying the bad word and was made to apologize to him. I was then sent to the camper for the rest of the day. I really thought my dad would have stood up for me especially when another grown man strikes your seven-year-old child. I don't know if dad ever spoke to him privately or not but I will never forget that day. I think this was the start of my rebellious stage. My family would still go camping and Skip and Diane would tag along, I on the other hand would go off by myself and fish. I loved to go fishing. Looking back at it now fishing was a good way for me to release some of my anxiety. I never had a conversation with Skip again.

I am really looking for my purpose.........well its really plain to see!

In 1967 dad retired from the Air Force after serving for 20+ years, NICE JOB DAD! We left South Dakota on another road trip, destination, Milford New Hampshire. Imagine this, a car full of kids under the age of ten with nothing but a bag of games and crayons. Try doing that today. Anyway, on this road trip we were pulling the camper. We were traveling during the winter time and all of a sudden one of the wheel bearings on the camper over heated and welded itself to the axle. We are having fun now! We were stranded on the side of the road with four kids ages 10, 9, 7, and 5, a car loaded with stuff and no where to go. We finally got some help from a man who was really nice. He had us back on our way in no time. We finally made it to Milford New Hampshire. We were all staying with my aunt Rita, my Meme' and a mean Chihuahua in a single wide trailer. All of us kids slept on the floor. Dad got a job with Coca Cola and after a couple of months my mom and dad bought a house. It was a nice 4 bedroom single family split level house in Merrimack New Hampshire. As I grew up it was very difficult for me to follow my brother Paul. Don't get me wrong I love my brother it was just hard to be number three. My sister Donna was number two. She was the first girl and I get it. Paul was always the one who could do no wrong. He was a Boy Scout and made it all the way to Eagle Scout. I never really cared for scouts. We all helped him with his eagle scout project and boy did we cut down a lot of trees that day. He was also a pretty good basketball player in High School and dad would go to his games when he could. Mom stayed home and took care of the rest of us. Paul became a Jr. Police Officer for the town of Merrimack and after a while he became what they called a Special Police Officer. They call them Auxiliary cops today. Then he went to the Police academy right out of high school and became a regular Police Officer soon afterwards. He was the youngest Police Officer in State history to graduate from the Police Academy. You could tell mom and dad were proud of him. I think we all were really. Dad had to buy his gun and ammo for him because he was not old enough to buy them, you had to be at least 21. I will say it was kinda cool to have a brother who was a Police Officer. Me on the other hand only wanted to work and to be with my friends. I was wondering away from my family. I wanted to have fun and have no responsibilities. I didn't care for high school at all and I was not a very good student. I'm sure if I had applied myself a little more I would have been better. When I was a freshman in high school I started working at a local grocery store, Ron's IGA, Ron Nenni was the owner. I worked for him until I graduated from high school. I bought my own car and now I had the means to be away from home. I never really felt like I belonged there. I was always getting in trouble. Not getting arrested trouble but teenage rebellious trouble, mostly towards my family. One time dad and I had a big fight and it was not good. He grabbed me around the neck and basically said it's time for you to leave. I did leave but not for very long. I came back later and apologized for my behavior, but I don't think the tension ever got better especially between me and Paul. Even today we don't have a close relationship. We get along but we don't talk much. I do wish our relationship was better. I played basketball when I was in Jr. high and high school, however I never did see dad at any of my games. After the games I usually had to walk home. It wasn't bad though I only lived about a mile (as the crow flies) from the school. Dad worked sometimes at night so if I wanted to play ball this is what I had to do. When I got my car I was able to drive to and from the games. Playing ball did force me to at least keep my grades at the passing level. My sister Donna and I were in the same grade, partly because I was held back in first grade. Donna was one of the popular kids at school. She was in clubs and was part of the class representatives. She was very popular at school and had a lot of friends. She is funny and very smart. Donna and I were probably in 9th grade or so when we had taken our blue jeans and cut the seams out on the legs and had sewn in bright colored material to make bell bottoms. Boy we had it going on then, long feathered hair, bell bottom jeans, wide collared shirts and red suede platform shoes. A Bee Gee hopeful. Yes I did!

I still have not found my purpose......are your eyes open?

High School graduation finally arrived, I actually had to get help from my girlfriends mom with a class project so I could graduate, Thanks Sheila! When I graduated I wasn't sure what I was going to do with my life. At one point I thought of being an architect but my grades were not good enough for continued education. I applied to a Tech school in Nashua NH but my high school math grades were not good enough and I did not qualify to go there. I struggled to find my place. I worked a few different jobs here and there, a mechanics helper, painter, glass cutter, service station worker and I even worked at a butcher shop de-boning chicken but I was never satisfied. I was never career minded until one day I decided to talk to an Air Force recruiter. Two things came to mind, a steady job would be good and a career started and dad would be proud of me for "following in his footsteps". The later however did not seem to be the case. When I came home and told my parents I was joining the Air Force I was asked when are you leaving? Not that's great, or congratulations, just, when are you leaving? I was a little disappointed but I understood why. I was not on good terms with them because of how I treated them. I have big regrets over that. I was sure they were ready for me to move on with my life. I signed up with a friend Tommy Papas. Tommy used to live in Chicago and his dad was a runner for the Chicago mafia. I found out about it when we went to Chicago during a spring break vacation. We had a great time and I met some very interesting people. Tommy and I were in the delayed enlistment program. We were going in the Air Force as buddies so we would be together during basic training. At the last minute Tommy had a family emergency in Chicago and could not go with me so I went by myself. I really had fun, well as much fun as basic training offered, but I missed my girlfriend Lonna and hanging with my friends. There were times of feeling lonely but basic got in the way pretty fast. I went in with a guaranteed job as a firefighter, after about two weeks in basic we all went to get our paperwork for our jobs and they told me the recruiter had made a mistake and my guaranteed job was not available. Now I had two choices. I could get out and go home or get a new job. I told them after shaving my head and yelling at me for two weeks I was not about to get out, I'll take another job. I was offered aircraft maintenance. So pardon the pun, I marched on to another change. I graduated from basic training and went to Sheppard AFB for more training.

Was this my purpose? Nope!

I had 10 weeks of training while I was at Sheppard AFB. Aircraft Maintenance was a great field and I knew right away I was going to like it. My first week there we were restricted to base and for good reason. The next week end we went off base to the local tavern which was right next door was a tattoo parlor. Guess what happened next. You got it and I got it, A TATOO. I don't even remember getting it. I woke up the next morning and there it was, a patch on my arm. My name and my girlfriend Lonna's name with an arrow through two hearts. We were not even married yet. This was without a doubt an alcohol related incident. Now I know why we were restricted to base the first week. Training was excellent and I knew the field I was going into would be a good one. Lonna and I actually planned to get married after I arrived at my first duty station. Training was now over and off to my first assignment.

On my own

My first assignment was at Laughlin AFB in Del Rio Texas. When I received my orders, I said where in the world is Del Rio Texas. I found it in the middle of nowhere on the boarder of Ciudad Acuna Mexico and Texas. Its ironic, when I joined the Air Force they told me "see the world and join the service". My first four years in the Air Force was in the great state of Texas. What a world. I hated it at first but I eventually began to enjoy being there. I guess I was getting comfortable with my job and meeting new people and making new friends. Lonna and I got married soon after I arrived in Del Rio. We were so young and very unaware of what life was about to give us. In June of 1978 we got married and we drove a 1969 Dodge Dart, loaded to the rafters with stuff, from Merrimack New Hampshire to Del Rio Texas, almost 2300 miles. When we got to Pennsylvania the exhaust system fell off, and when I say fell off I mean fell off. The muffler and the exhaust pipe were dragging on the ground. So now a stop at a muffler shop. A few welds later and we were back on our way. The muffler shop guy was great. He found out we were newlyweds and so he did the work for free. Our plan was to share the driving and drive straight through. Well we were making good time and then in Virginia the transmission went out. As we pulled off the interstate there was, low and behold, a transmission repair place right there. So now we had to get it fixed. **THIS IS NOT OVER!** We get into Arkansas and the car overheats. The only thing we could do at this point was to laugh, and we did. We finally arrived in Del Rio. I was able to get us a nice apartment and we were excited to get our life started. We had a lot of parties with most of them keg parties. Like we could afford it! Sometime we would drive across the border and get a few bottles of Mezcal Tequila, you know the one with the worn inside, those were some crazy parties. We did not have a care in the world and all we wanted to do was have fun. I did not make a lot of money being in the military and we lived pay check to paycheck most of the time. The fun began to play a toll on both of us. Arguments about money and Lonna not having anything to do was a constant thing. I remember when we would have a couple of days left before I would get paid and we had no money and very little food in the house. We would donate blood at the local blood bank so we would have enough money until I got paid again. After a couple of years went by Lonna got a job working at a bar called The Stagecoach Inn. This was definitely not a good idea. Things got much worse when this happened.

Not my purpose yet!...your not ready to see it.

Sheila: Translated to the Hebrew name Ora, it means Light

Arguments and having no money was a constant battle. I was tired of dealing with it and something needed to give, then Lonna became pregnant. Now we were asking ourselves how are we going to afford a child. We learned to manage our money better and in January 1980, one of the greatest days of my life had arrived, my daughter Sheila was born. She was and is as beautiful as ever. When the nurse handed her to me she was crying up a storm but as soon as I had her in my arms she stopped crying. I looked at the nurse and said "that's my girl"....we laughed. It was a long day for both of us. Lonna was a trooper. She was in labor for over seventeen long hours and eventually she had to have a C-section because Sheila was breach. I tried to help her with her lamas breathing but I ended up having to leave, or should I say asked to leave, the delivery room because I was starting to hyperventilate. In my defense though I had been up with no sleep for over 30 hours at this point. Breathing into a paper bag and then an oxygen mask was not my idea of fun. However the pilots I worked with had a good time with it. Some of their wife's were nurses in the delivery room and they told them what had happened. I was greeted, for about a week, with barf bags and was loudly offered oxygen from the aircraft so I would feel better. It was a bunch of fun to interact with the Officers in this way. I was also thrown into the SOLO pool for the birth of my daughter by the pilots. It was a great honor to be recognized by them in this way. That pool was reserved for special occasions for officers not enlisted personnel. Things between Lonna and I improved a little because now we have someone else to think about. We had moved into a bigger apartment and it was a little bit cheaper which helped our finances. Our finances were limited and Lonna always wanted to go back to New Hampshire. She would go back from time to time, even though we could not afford it, but I wanted her to be happy. When she would come back she would be fine for awhile but then she became home sick again and wanted to go back again. She was not happy.

We finally were able to get into base housing and we lived about two blocks from our friends, Richard and Julia. Lonna was excited about it and living on base gave us some relief from the financial burden of rent and utilities. We finally had a chance to settled down. We even had some extra money so

Lonna did not need to work anymore. We could now concentrate on raising Sheila. No more parties. At times we would go over to Richard and Julia's house and have a few drinks but not like before. Richard and I would play our guitars and the girls would sing along and laugh. Mainly at me and Richard. Coming into Los Angeles was our favorite song to play. Things were going great and soon Lonna was pregnant again. The second greatest day of my life came in November 1981. It would be the birth of my second child. She was going to come into this world but on her own terms. Lonna was dealing with Pre-eclampsia and so she was admitted to the hospital early. Lonna began having contractions but they were several minutes apart. Lonna at the time was sitting up playing cards with our friend Julia. The nurses said it would be awhile before the baby was born so I left the hospital with Sheila in tow. I took Sheila home and sat her in her high chair and I put a bowl of spaghetti-O's in front of her, then the phone rings. **It's a girl!** is what I heard when I answered the phone. I said no way I missed it? Julia was with Lonna at the time when my daughter was born. When I got back to the hospital we were wondering what to name the newest member of our family and I said why don't we name her Julia. Julia had came by to visit Lonna while I was gone with Sheila and she helped her through the delivery. The doctor told me she came so fast and even if they had called me to come back I would not have made it back for the delivery. He said she came out so fast it was like spitting out a piece of bubble gum. Julia was so excited that she would be her namesake and so we now have another family member and her name is……..Julia.

Julia: Translated to the Hebrew name Nima, it means Blessing

Was this my purpose now? Not exactly!

There were turbulent times in our marriage. The best times were between our two girls being born and us going to the UK. When I received orders to go to England, RAF Lakenheath to be precise, we were both apprehensive about the move. I was unsure about Lonna. She was not happy being a military wife and we were doing pretty good at this point. I went to the UK and had settled in to my new post. I was able to get us housing rather quickly so I sent for Lonna and the kids. When they arrived I was very happy to have them there. We were starting a new chapter in our lives in a far away land. The first few months were great. We met some really nice people in our neighborhood and it seemed as though things would be good. Unfortunately the long hours and me being away a lot paid a toll on Lonna. I believe she was lonely and wanted someone or anyone to pay attention to her. She strayed and the next thing I know our marriage was now on the rocks....again. Then to make matters worse I had to leave on a lengthy TDY (temporary duty) to RAF Sculthorpe due to the runway at Lakenheath needing to be redone. The TDY was for ten to twelve months and I was gone for almost all of it. Lonna had to take care of the kids and do most of the work by herself. This did not help our marriage at all. Not a good time for her. I'm not saying her transgression were justified but she was lonely. Lonna needed my help and because I was away I couldn't give it to her. Being a military wife was a hard job but Lonna did not help her cause any. She would call my supervisor and yell at him telling him to let me come home and help her. I must have been called into his office a dozen times telling me to have her stop. My squadron commander was even notified. I was advised by him and I quote "she had better stop calling us or I will have her sent back to the states". This was not good. I spoke to Lonna about the calls, I told her what would happen and asked her to stop. The calls stopped for a while but when I could not come home on a specific weekend because I was the on call Non Commissioned Officer in Charge, she blew up and made a call directly to my first sergeant. Guess what happened next. Within a month my Commander had pulled her sponsorship, drafted orders, packed up our house and had her sent back to the states. I could not do anything to stop it. I was not even allowed to escort her and the kids to the airport. I was under orders to not leave the base. I watched my wife and kids leave on a bus from a parking lot on base. I never thought this would happen but it did. I somehow felt like I may have been able to avoid it but I later realized it was not possible. The word divorce was said to me as she was getting on the bus.

My purpose....where are you?

Lonna and the kids were back in the states and I was devastated. I am still at Sculthorpe. Lonna and I spoke on the phone and she told me she filed for a divorce. I cried for some time. I felt my world had shattered and was falling apart. Not having my kids around me was the saddest part. I love them dearly. I miss them and now I was the lonely one. Believing I was getting divorced I went looking for some companionship. I had met this young lady who was from the area. Her name was Susan. We really hit it off. Neither of us wanted a sexual relationship only companionship which was great. I was hoping Lonna and I would reconcile and I did not want to commit to any other relationship. I wanted to remain faithful. After a few months though Susan and I started to want more. Lonna was still saying we are divorcing and so I finally said I am going to move on with my life. Susan and I took our relationship to the next level. We began to get a bit more serious and before we knew it I love you's were in the air. We have not slept together yet and I would sometimes feel guilty about our relationship. Even during this time I was being told there was no hope for our marriage and we needed to divorce. I was on duty one night when Lonna called. One of my coworkers answered the phone and said your wife is on the phone and she said it was an emergency. When I answered it she said she was in London and I needed to come and get her and the kids. At first I thought she was joking but she was not. I now had to go to London from Sculthorpe which was about an 8 hour drive and get them. I did not even have a place for them to stay. I was living in the barracks. My boss was furious and reminded me of what happened last time. I had to wait until my shift was over because my boss was "not going to wake up anyone for my drama". Quote unquote. At 7am I was on my way to Lakenheath and was taking the bus to London Heathrow airport. I will admit once I saw them I was happy they were there. I really missed them. We took the bus back to Lakenheath and I was able to get them into the on base quarters for two weeks. I found us a place to live and we were back together. Lonna told me she was mad at me and wanted me to feel bad. She never filed for a divorce. Now I had to tell Susan. It was hard because we did love each other. Susan was not happy but she understood. I will always cherish our time together. My love for my family was stronger. Lonna and I had to readjust and learn to trust each other again. With Lonna having an an affair and me having a relationship with another woman while we were separated was a bit hard to bare for both of us. It would take time for trust to re-enter our lives. I was worried she may call my boss again and I reminded her of what happened the last time she was here, she didn't make any more calls. My younger sister Kathy joined us in the UK and was our live in nanny. Lonna got a job on base at the dentist office. I guess after she reads this she will know, but the dentist she worked for was the pilot who flew my jet. He asked me about her and I told him she would do well. He was familiar with the issues we were having before she came back. I told him I wanted her to get the job on her own merits not mine. He hired her and later told me it was the best thing he had done. We spent the last year in England as a family who worked hard at mending the fences. I played semi-professional darts and would travel locally to tournaments. Lonna would go with me to some of my dart matches I would have. During our separation while Lonna was still in the states, I had won the Barningham district tournament and then played a practice round in London with the world champion Eric Bristow. We played three games. He won the first, I won the second and he waxed me on the third. He was great and fun to meet. Not too many people can say they drank a beer, in London, with the world champion of darts. I still worked a lot of hours but they were mostly days so I was able to be home in the evenings. That made things so much nicer.

Is it my purpose time yet? Not yet!

We left the UK as a happy family. The military was sending me to Columbus Mississippi. Columbus AFB is another Air Training Command base. I really wanted an assignment closer to home but you know the military, they come first. We were in New Hampshire for two weeks before I left to go to Mississippi. I was worried Lonna would not follow me there. She was back at home with her mom and she seemed very content being there. My father-in-law Bob and I drove a 1972 Chevrolet Nova to Little Rock where he lived and then I drove it the rest of the way to Mississippi. I liked him and we got along great. One day on our trip Bob was driving and we got pulled over in Indiana by the Indiana State Police. I had been sleeping and I asked him what he had done and he said I don't know. The next thing we knew we were being asked to get out of the car over the patrol cars PA system and were being held at gun point...seriously! After being put in hand cuffs and standing on the side of the interstate for 45 minutes we were released. We were told there was an armed robbery at a truck stop about ten miles back. The robbers were two white males and the get away car was a blue and white nova. Guess what we were in? When we were released we did not stop until we got out of Indiana.....and I drove.

Once in Mississippi I again settled into my job and was able to get housing rather quickly. We had a great three bedroom house on base. I could walk to work in 10 minutes. I sent for Lonna and the kids and after a few weeks of being there she started to complain. She tried to find a job but was unsuccessful. Then Lonna's dad was involved in a plane crash. He was a pilot and was training a student when the student froze while they were practicing stalls and would not let go of the yoke. The plane took a nose dive at the end of the runway. Lonna went back to New Hampshire and stayed for awhile. In fact she was gone so long I had to move out of base housing and back into the barracks. Her dad was in bad shape and fortunately he survived. When Lonna was ready to come back I applied for base housing and when I got a house she came back. Lonna came back but she was never the same. I did not know how to fix her pain. I could only watch her decline. She began going out by herself and then eventually she strayed again. To make a long story short she left for New Hampshire this time with another guy. At this point I am feeling like I can't do or get anything done right to please her. I moved back into the barracks and now my marriage was over. I was sending her as much money as I could but it did not seem to be enough. Bad checks were being written by her and I had to close my account to stop from getting in trouble with my commanders. What a mess. Things could not get any worse when I was told the base was going to be operated by civilian personnel and all active duty personnel in maintenance would be shipped out within a year. Re-enlistment time was around the corner and I had a decision to make. Then.....guess what. I am at work on the flight line and was in the middle of turning the aircraft for more flights when I get called off the flight line and taken to the commander's office. He tells me a report was taken about me and it needed immediate attention. It was said I was going to kill myself. I'm like WHAT! My commander said the report came from my wife who said I was so distraught by her leaving me and there was no way I was going to live without her. I was blown away by this. I now had to get evaluated to make sure I didn't off myself. What an adventure that was.

Surely my purpose was now known! No....again.

Time now to make a decision. Do I re-enlist or get out? I had an opportunity to get an early out and go back home. I did have a job lined up if I wanted it with the fire department in Merrimack. All I had to do was pass the physical agility test. That was not going to be a problem. Well I made my decision to get out early and go home. My thought was maybe my marriage could still be saved, or at the least I will be near my kids. So out of the service and off to New Hampshire.

Jeremiah 29:11 For I know the plans I have for you, declares the Lord, plans to prosper you and not to harm you, plans to give you hope and a future.

Reflection In her defense

Now I want to pause here for a second or two and come to Lonna's defense. It seems up to this point I am bashing her and running her through the mud. This is not the case. I want to be clear, we were both to blame for our marriage going south. We were very young and foolish when we got married. Lonna had just turned 17 and I just turned 21.   Neither of us made good decisions especially when it came to our finances and the military life is a very harsh and sometimes brutal life especially for spouses. My time away from her was sometimes voluntary but we needed the money and the TDY pay was really good. I should have made a better decision about leaving her alone. God had a plan for both of us but we did not know it yet.

Any sign of my purpose yet?...Really you just asked that again!

New beginnings

So here I am back in New Hampshire and living with dear old mom and dad. Don t get me wrong I am grateful they wanted me home but I am used to being on my own, not living with my parents. I had all of the paperwork filled out for the fire department and a date to take the physical agility test. It was a waiting game now. I was trying to reconcile with Lonna and save our marriage. I was naive to think with another man now in her life I was going to save anything, but I still wanted to try. I was in New Hampshire for about two weeks with no progress and there wasn't going to be any. I saw it now. We were arguing so much it was impossible to even meet with her and speak with her rationally. My parents saw the pain I was in and offered to help with the finances of a lawyer. I spoke with him and advised him to go ahead and file for the divorce. I needed to leave New Hampshire and I had a friend who I was stationed with at Columbus AFB who lived in Georgia,. He offered me a place to stay if I could not work things out with my marriage. I needed to make a change so I called him and asked him if the offer still stood, he said yes sir come on down. Lonna and I met at Pizza Hut one more time, I could have tried to plea my case as to why we should try and work things out but I knew now things were not going to change. I gave Lonna most the money I had, gave my kids a hug and kiss and off to Georgia I went. I really felt like my life was over and I was at my wits end. I had no job, no future and the people I loved the most was now gone from my life. Driving away from my family and seeing them in my rear view mirror had to be one of the hardest things I ever had to do. I was not sure how I was going to cope with not having them around. Eventually I found the best coping mechanism ever.

Psalm 27:1 The Lord is my light and my salvation-whom shall I fear? The Lord is the stronghold of my life-of whom shall I be afraid?

I arrived at my friends house and was now in a place I was not familiar with. I lived in Stockbridge Georgia and my first priority was finding work. I was able to find a job pretty quick. I was hoping I would get on with the airlines but I needed a job quickly so I took the first one I found. It was an assistant manager position in shipping at Carolina Pottery. This job was a hold out job until I could get on with the airlines. I went to most of the airlines in Atlanta but unfortunately the airline industry was going through some turbulent times. Eastern Airlines was on the brink of a strike and most of their mechanics were bailing and going to other airlines. I on the other hand was working but not making enough money to support my self especially when I was sending most of my money to Lonna to help support the kids. I had a good friend who left Carolina Pottery and went to work for Kmart as their lost prevention manager. He called me and said Kmart paid better and was looking for a patio manager and he recommended me for the job. The store manager offered me the job so I left Carolina Pottery and went to work for Kmart. I was still waiting for a phone call from the airlines. I waited almost 6 months and no calls. I spoke to the store manager about getting a bit more money and he said the Fayetteville Georgia store was looking for a lost prevention manager. The pay was a lot better but I would have to transfer to Fayetteville. So I took the position and off to Fayetteville I go. The job did pay better and I was able to get my own apartment. Loss prevention was a nice job. It had some excitement with catching shoplifters and working on internal theft issues. I met a young lady named Lori who worked at the store as their customer service representative. As time went on and we got to know each other better and I finally asked her if she wanted to go out for dinner one night and she accepted. We got along really well. As we talked I found out she was looking for an apartment. She had a daughter from her first marriage and she wanted to move out from her mothers and find a place of her own. My apartment had two bedrooms and I thought we could become roommates. I had been living there for a few months alone so I felt It would help both of us financially and it sounded like a good idea. So after about a month or so of us knowing each other she moved in as my roommate. Well...not for very long anyway. My divorce had been final for awhile and so my roommate became my girlfriend. After a few months we ended up sleeping together and once that happened we decided to get married. I transferred from Fayetteville to the Forest Park store and we had the go ahead to get married. With me being in management we couldn't work at the same store. My friends thought it was too soon and even my best man was saying he did not care for Lori, there was something about her he could not put his finger on. He said he would stand with me though if I still wanted him to. We got married. Now I'm in my second marriage.

Okay, this has to be a sign that my purpose is here.....Ugh no!

Looking back now it was not a good idea AT ALL. We had fun together and partied a lot. She took a promotion and started working in the pharmacy as one of the techs. Now here is where things start getting interesting. Lori had three children one who lived with her before we got married. Then afterwards another child moved in with us. They were very sweet and well behaved. I think they liked me. We did have to move because our little two bedroom apartment got small really quick. We rented a small house with three bedrooms and started to really like the house. We put a new roof on it and started to fix it up. The owner was interested in selling the house to us but we were not ready to take the plunge yet. Then Lonna called and asked me if I would take the girls for awhile. Her sister and boyfriend were living in the same house as her and the girls. They were doing drugs and Lonna did not want the girls around this behavior. She was having trouble finding an apartment and could not afford one at the time so she asked would I take the girls. I of course said yes and within a week both Sheila and Julia were living with me. I was so excited. The house now was too small so we ended up renting, with an option to own, a double wide trailer from my new brother-in-law. It was four bedrooms and three full baths. Perfect for our now large family. It was pretty nice but needed some carpentry work done on the inside. I was able to do all the work at a reduced rate on our rent. Then it began to happened.

Lori's family was extremely "religious". They went to a small independent Baptist church and were always asking us to join them on Sundays. I was not at all interested. I respected them for their beliefs but was not going to be one of those "Bible Thumpers". I actually said it. We always met for Sunday dinner at my mother-in-laws house. She made the best Collards and corn bread I ever had. From time to time though my brother-in-law would still ask us to join them at church and the answer was always no thanks.

I received a call from the store manager of Mervyns Department store who offered me a chance to go into their management program for the company and then later become a district manager. The money was slightly higher and the opportunity was much greater. I still have not heard from the airlines. Eastern at this time went under and the industry was at a standstill. I accepted the job and started work right away. Then it happened. Lori began to drink. When I say drink I mean drink. We started to argue a lot and did not see eye to eye on just about everything. We both drank but her drinking was a bit excessive. She actually started to hide it from me so I would think she had stopped. It did not at all.

I was surprised with a phone call from a friend who worked for Henry County Sheriffs office. He asked me to come by and see him. When I spoke with him he said an opening had come up and he put my name in for it. The job was working in the jail, but later it would be possible for me to go to the Police Academy and go to the road as a Deputy. I scheduled my interview and afterwards I was hired on with the Sheriffs Office. WOW what a change in jobs. First wanting to work for the airlines and now Law Enforcement. I was really excited. I called my brother to tell him. This was his response "I don't think you have the right temperament for the job and it will never work for you". I thought he would be excited for me and would encourage me in this new endeavor. Not quite.

Okay, so my purpose is in sight now, right?

Not exactly.

Lori was not happy. She was not a "Pro Police person" and did not want her husband in Law Enforcement. I told her the job would be good for my carrier and the benefits and retirement would be great for us in the long run. She still was not happy. She would make fun of me when I would come out dressed in my uniform. She began to drink more and now she was not hiding it. I tried everything to help her with this problem but she would not accept it. At least she wasn't drinking and then going to work. That I knew of anyway.

Born again!

My Brother-in-law would come over from time to time, mostly on Tuesday nights when his sister was working. He started this right after I got married to his sister. He would talk with me about Jesus. He would bring his bible and would read passages from it and then explain them to me. I was glad to have the company. I had made a comment to him one time during one of his visits if I had a bible I would probably read it. On his next visit he had a bible for me. We would talk for a couple of hours or so and then he would pray for me and then leave. One day he came by the house and he did not have his bible with him. He told me he was only going to stay for a short while. He said he wanted to ask me a few questions and then he would be leaving. I felt like he was angry with me for some reason but it was not the case at all. His first question was "what happens to a stick if I was to put it in mud then take it out and put it to the side"? I said the mud would eventually dry. He then said "what happens if I did the same same thing day in and day out over thirty years or so"? I said the stick would be caked with mud. He said "you are the stick". He said now "what would happen if I took the stick and put it in a clean pool of water and swirled it around day in and day out"? I said the mud would eventually soften and fall off. He said "Jesus is the water". Now all I am asking you to do is "GET IN THE WATER". If you don't like it then you can get out, but I promise you if you stay the course and trust in Him you will like it and you won't get out. He then stood up and started to leave. I was really thinking now maybe he has something here. He told me Jesus can solve and help with all my problems and when you have troubles He will walk with you and I would never be alone. I watched him walk out the door and I followed him and said Okay what do I need to do to "get in the water". He said you need to say the sinners prayer and then publicly profess your faith and get baptized. I said Okay I'm in. So he and I got on our knees in my driveway and I accepted Jesus as my Lord and Savior. I was shaking all over but when I stood up the first thing I saw was the smile on my brother-in-laws face. I can say now I really did feel different. We went back inside and read the bible some more and his encouragement to me was awesome. His sister on the other hand laughed when I told her what had happened. I went to church the next Wednesday and then on Sunday where I got baptized. Lori actually got baptized with me but her relationship with Jesus didn't last long. I don't usually commit to do something unless I can be fully committed. I wanted and needed a change in my life and this was it. I was committed to see this through. FOREVER! Besides.....How bad can this Jesus thing be anyway. Later I found out it was the best thing I had ever done! Born again!

Is my purpose going to be shown to me now?

Through Jesus?.....Possibly

After about 10 months at Henry County Sheriffs Office, the Sheriff began having problems with the County commissioners, in the end 33 Officers were laid off. I was one of them and I was devastated. The Sheriff had called me to his office and told me he had a spot for me at the Academy but if I wanted to go I would have to pay for it. I told him I would go. I actually got pretty lucky. I was able to get my old job back at Mervyns and was able to work my schedule around going to the Academy. I was determined now to make this Police thing work. I really liked it. So while I worked at Mervyns I was able to go to the Academy. The classes were at night and on Saturdays mornings. About two weeks before I graduated I was called out of the classroom by one of the lieutenants and was escorted to her office. I sat down and she handed me an application for the

Fayetteville Police Department. She told me they were hiring and she had recommended me for the position. She said I had done really well and was going to graduate at or near the top of my class. She told me to fill out the application and get it back to her on the next day. I filled it out and returned it to her the next day and within two weeks I had an interview. I graduated the Academy and finished second in my class by one quarter of a point. How does that happen. I started praying that I would see Gods will and to deliver me from not having a stable job, to stabilize my marriage and deliver me from smoking and drinking. To allow me to see my sins and ask for forgiveness of those sins and to help me be strong through it all.

1 John 5:14-15 This is the confidence we have in approaching God; that if we ask anything according to His will, He will hear us.

The Chief of Police for Fayetteville PD was Ed Lynch, what a great Chief. I respected him dearly. A good Christian man with common sense values. When I had my interview with him he knew I was nervous, so he sat in a chair next to me, not with a table or desk between us, he made me feel as comfortable as possible. We spoke for a few minutes and he asked me questions about my family and where I was from. He was looking at my record from the Academy and was impressed I had finished near the top of my class and I wanted to be an officer so bad I paid my own way through the academy. When my interview was almost over Chief Lynch asked me my final question, "if I hired you how are you going to treat the citizens of Fayetteville"? I told him I would treat them the way I would want to be treated. How cliche, but I really meant it and he knew it. He told me he had another interview but to call him at 1 o'clock and he would let me know of his decision. My interview was at 9am and I must say it was the longest 4 hours of my life. When I called at 1pm Chief Lynch said I have one more question, when can you start? I was so excited! My interview was on Friday November 8, 1991 and I started on Monday November 11, 1991.

Yea my purpose is here now I am certain of it...Don't kid yourself.

A fresh start

On my first day at the Police Department I had to go get my uniforms and all of my equipment. I had to provide my own gun too because the department could not afford to issue me one. Once I was in uniform I went back to the station to get sworn in. I felt like I was invincible. My training officer was Sgt. David Bailey. He and I really hit it off. We had some of the same hobbies, we like to play golf, carpentry work, fishing and we both had a love for Jesus. He gave me a small pocket cross on my first day on the job and I still have it in my pocket today. We actually look like we could be brothers. David's wife had actually waived me down one time and when I pulled over to speak with her she said "Oh I thought you were David never mind". We laughed. David and I spoke about Jesus quite a bit and he was a good person to talk to about the issues I was having in my marriage. As time went on though Lori still resented me being a Police Officer and would always talk bad about the profession. She didn't like my relationship with Jesus either. She would start laughing when I would try and talk with her about it. She would sometimes make comments about how God was cruel and mean and he would never do anything for her. She would even cuss at me and God when I would ask her to go with me to church. I decided it would be better to let her want what I had by seeing how happy I was with Jesus. Then Lonna called me one day and said she had found an apartment and was able to keep Sheila and Julia away form the situation they had previously been living in and was now wanting to get the girls back She asked could the kids come back and I told her only if they wanted to. The girls wanted to go back and I found out later why the girls wanted to go back. Lori was abusing them, physically and mentally. She told the girls if they said anything to me she would punish them. I didn't find this out until Mary and I were married. If I had known what she was doing to them earlier she would have been out on her ear. After a couple of months went by I was working an extra duty job when Lori showed up and was crying. I asked her what the problem was and she said she had run over a dog and was upset about it. She said the dog had ran off and she couldn't find it to see if it was

Okay. I told her I was sorry for her hitting the animal and I would talk to her more about it when I got home. The job ended at midnight and when I got home she was not there. Her truck was gone and most of her clothes were also gone. Now, I am not sure what to think at this point. I called the hospital, jails and she was not there. I called her mom and my brother-in-law and she was not there either. I started to worry, I stayed up for the majority of the night. The next morning she called me and told me she was leaving me and was going back to her ex-husband. She did not want to be married to a cop. I was blown away and didn't see this coming. She admitted to having an affair with her Ex and was doing so the entire time we were married. Now I'm mad. I started to think "another failed marriage". I started to wonder how God felt about divorce. I didn't want to deal with another woman who has committed adultery. I spoke to my pastor about it and he told me to pray about it. I told him I was but I was not hearing a response to what I needed to do. I was a new christian, about a year or so, and I was not sure how I needed to handle this situation. I was really struggling with this because I knew how God felt about divorce. I tried to make contact with Lori and she would not speak to me. I left her a message saying God would not be pleased if we divorced. After a couple of days she called me and told me I could take my God and put it where the sun does not shine. I was like Okay now this is the last straw. I spoke to my pastor again and he told me to have faith and God will work it out. I was starting to doubt my pastor was any help for me with this. My brother-in-law saw I was having trouble with just being told to pray and so he came by to see me. He told me he loved his sister but he loved Jesus more and so he showed me in the bible where even though Jesus did not like divorce there are some cases it would be Okay.

Mathew 19:9 I tell you that anyone who divorces his wife, <u>except for sexual immorality,</u> and marries another woman commits adultery.

I was grateful for his council and it made me feel better about my decision. My wife was not coming back and she was not someone who was going to waste their time going to church. She was now living with her ex-husband and so I made the decision to Divorce her. I filed for a divorce and within a month or so we were divorced.

Not sure about my purpose.......Just wait!

I made a decision to focus on my work and not so much on another relationship. My main focus was God and work. I prayed every day if God wanted me in a relationship He would provide someone for me. I asked for someone who would Love me for who I am not for what I can give them. I wanted her to Love the Lord as much as I did.

Deuteronomy 6:5 Love the Lord with all your heart and with all your soul and with all strength.

Jesus said in:

John 15:7 If you remain in me, and my words remain in you, ask whatever you wish, and it will be done for you.

Okay…...I dated a few times and was not very satisfied about how these relationships were going. None felt right. Some felt down right wrong. One wanted to get married and we only dated twice. She was a nice girl but I ran from her. Then one day my dispatcher called me to the department to take a report and when I was finished I walked out to get into my patrol car and another one of my dispatchers was in the parking lot with a friend. She had been telling me about this friend of hers and wanted us to meet. I was really not interested but decided to be nice and meet her. When I introduced myself to her I felt this person was special. I wasn't sure how or why only she was special. Her name was Mary. She was beautiful and had really pretty blue eyes. They were kind and gentle and I liked that a lot. We exchanged phone numbers and I told her if she wanted to go out to call me and we can schedule a date. I got into my patrol car and went back to work. During the course of the night I could not stop thinking about her. I know I prayed for someone but was God telling me this was her. At this point in my life I was not really interested in a relationship but I could not stop thinking about her so I called her. It was late in the evening and I was not sure if she would even be up. She was still up and I asked her if she wanted to go out. She said Okay and we set a date. I told her I got off at 11pm and if she was still up I would like to call her back and talk with her for awhile. She said it would be fine. I got off at 11 and went straight home. I called her and we spoke on the phone for about an hour talking about our work and things. I was very comfortable with her. Our first date was an early movie and then dinner. We met at the theater and saw Lethal Weapon 2. Later I found out she was not crazy about action movies but she was Okay with this because she knew I liked them. We went to dinner at Ruby Tuesdays at the Mall and we both ordered the same thing. As our date progressed we nailed down the particulars. We said if we were to go forward with this relationship we may as well tell each other what we wanted from this relationship. We both wanted the same thing. First to love God, then each other, no monetary desires beyond our control and no fighting and no drinking. We talked about our previous relationships and we were both fine with knowing about them. We ended our date in the parking lot with what we call now a "parking lot kiss". When I went home I thanked God for her and went to sleep. It was probably the best nights sleep I have had in a great while.

Mary: *In Hebrew it means beloved*

Is she my purpose? Well.............Not really.

As our relationship went on, we must have seen each other 5 out of 7 days a week and we really like being with each other. Then we began to fall in love. We both thought this was crazy because we had only known each other for a short period of time but we also felt God does work in mysterious ways. We truly believed God had brought us together for a reason. We thought things were going good but our families felt we were moving too fast. Neither of us was looking for a permanent relationship so our focus was to put God first and see what He was going to do with this relationship. Every time we would do something with our relationship it was confirmed in such a way that we knew we were on the right track and it was from God. One day I was talking to her kids, Jennifer and CJ, about our relationship. I wanted them to know I did not want to take their dads place. I wanted them to have a good relationship with him, but I really like their mom and what did they think about it. Both were very happy we were together and they could tell we loved each other. Now think about this for one moment. We never told them we love each other and they saw our relationship as love. What a powerful confirmation on our feelings towards each other. Later I asked Jennifer and CJ for their mothers hand in marriage and I got a big yes from them. We were going to wait and get Married in the summer of the following year but later we said what are we waiting for, we loved each other, we are going to get married so we decided to do it early. September 19, 1992 was the beginning of a new chapter in both of our lives. *Mark 10:9*

Therefore what God has joined together, let no

one separate.

A brand new walk

We were very happy about our decision. We found us a church right a way and we bought our first house in 1993. We had our ups and downs when it came to Lonna and the kids. Lonna and I would have arguments on the phone about me seeing the kids. I was not wanting this in my life anymore. I had enough of it when we were married and I certainly did not want this now. It was not my life anymore. It was rough at first but eventually things started to settle down and we became more civil with each other. Things with our marriage were going great. Not only were we growing together as husband and wife but also with the Lord. CJ and Jennifer were plugged in with their youth group and they seemed very happy there. One Sunday we were in Sunday school and our teacher was asking the class to give donations to a family to help with costs for a lawyer due to another class member being in jail. We were told the member was in jail for supposedly extortion and needed money for a new trial. The class member was put in isolation and was not allowed to speak with other inmates. I was surprised to hear this behavior. I worked in a jail and the only reason we would separate inmates was if they didn't get along or there was a crime against either a child or a spouse. This bothered me so I made contact with an Assistant DA I knew and he told me because the case had been adjudicated he could tell me what happened. He said the person in question was in jail for Aggravated Child molestation. He had abused his own children. Hence we have been lied to. This did not sit well with me and so I spoke to our Sunday school teacher and advised him of this new information. He was floored by this news. I told him the class needed to know and if he didn't tell them I would. I can't belong to a church Sunday school class who is being lied to and this needed to be set right. He agreed. Next Sunday he did not tell the class he came in and resigned as the teacher and then left the church. The class was told by someone else. After this incident Mary and I were basically shunned from the class. We would come in on Sunday and no one would speak to us or sit next to us. I told Mary we need to stop coming to this class. We went to a couple of other classes but never really felt welcome. One day a new Youth pastor came to the church and at first he seemed Okay. After awhile though he began to have confidential meetings with the kids. Meetings the kids were not allowed to speak about, especially with their parents. Mary and I were youth leaders there and we attended a meeting with the youth. The meeting was about a trip the kids were taking to Panama City Fl. He made the comment that the girls were to wear T-shirts over their bathing suit because if they didn't he would lust over them. I was blown away. I asked him to clarify his statement and he said well what I meant was he was like all men would be tempted by the flesh and they needed to be a bit more modest with what they were wearing. We were not very happy about this. We spoke to the Senior pastor about it and he said if we did not like it we could pull our kids out of the group. We spoke to the kids about it and explained our feelings about what was going on They assured us things were not bad and we should trust them to make the right decisions with this matter. This was against our better judgment but we also felt the kids were good and we should trust them. We did however ask Jennifer to speak with a friend of mine who worked with me at the Police Department. If she told me things were Okay then I would take her advise and stop worrying. The interview went well and we were told we did not have anything to be concerned with so we dropped the matter.

Psalm 32:8 I will instruct you and teach you in the way you should go; I will counsel you with my loving eye on you.

Things went pretty good afterwards. Mary and I had moved to Fayetteville to be closer to my work. We wanted a new house in a better area. We found this house and only God could have done for us what was done. We found this house and really wanted it. We had a contract on our old house but the guy wanting to buy the house was trying to sell it before he even bought it. We told him to buy the house first then sell it and he was not happy with what we told him so he pulled his contract. We had put a contract on our new house but now we were in jeopardy of loosing it. Our real estate agent called me and asked us to come by to speak with him, he had a solution to our problem. When we sat down he told us he wanted to buy my house and he was going to give us what we were asking for it. He told us he did not want us to loose the other house and so he was going to buy mine. I told him he did not have to do this and he said he knew but he wanted to. We closed on both of the properties and we moved into our new home.

Psalm 9:10 Those who know your name trust in you, for you, Lord, have never forsaken those who seek you.

We were now in our forever home. CJ was living with his dad and Jennifer stayed with us for awhile. Later she moved in with her dad to finish out her senior year in high school and then go on to college. We were now empty nesters. We missed having the kids around but later on we began to adjust to the quiet.

I am not seeing my purpose. You are absolutely right!

A captive audience...Kind of!

As Christians we always have chances to witness. As a Police Officer I sometimes would have a captive audience, so to speak. While at work one day I was asked to go to south Georgia to pick up a prisoner that we had warrants on. The trip was going to take about six hours to go down get him and then come back. On our way back I was around Macon on I75 when the prisoner asked me what I was listening to on the radio. I told him it was a christian radio station He asked me if I would put it on the rear speakers so I put it on the rear speakers and after awhile he started asking questions, are you a christian, how long have you been a christian, what has it done for you and so on. He started to tell me his story about how he never had a good life and he felt like there was always something missing. He could never find his place. He said he was so tired of being in and out of jail and he wanted his life to change. I could tell he wanted this. I told him Christ can help him but he would have to change his ways. We spoke the rest of the way about Jesus and how he helped me. When we got to the jail and was inside the gate, I stopped the car and had him get out, I took the handcuffs off and we prayed together for his salvation and he accepted Christ on that day. I just could not pray for a man in the back of a patrol car who was in hand cuffs for his salvation. I put the cuffs back on and took him inside. He was smiling from ear to ear. The jailer even asked why are you smiling and he said I just found Jesus. What an amazing day this was.

A life saved

One day while on patrol I received a call for service to go to an apartment complex on a possible suicide call. When I arrived on scene I made contact with the resident who stated he was going to kill himself. I was talking to him through the front door. He was extremely upset and at times you could tell he was crying. There was a shakiness in his voice. He told me he had lost his job that he really liked and then a week later his girlfriend left him. She told him he was worthless for loosing his job and she would not stay with a man who can't give his girlfriend what she wanted. While I was speaking with him I continued to pray God would give me the words to say to this young man which would end this situation and to be able to get him the help he deserves. I told him his life was important and he had everything to live for. I told him God wants to help him, he sees his potential and worth. I kept asking him to open the door and let me speak with him face to face and eventually he opened the door. This took about two and a half hours. When I walked in I did not see a gun. I asked him did he have one and he said yes he had put it on the bed. My partner went and retrieved it. Then we sat down on his sofa and I spoke with him for another hour or so. We were able to make contact with his mom and she was now on her way to our location. While we were waiting for her I asked him did he have a church pastor who could come and speak with him and he said no. I invited him to join me on Sunday and I would try and get him plugged in there. I told him to contact me when he got home and then I would take him to church with me on Sunday. He said he would like that and it would be nice. He was very grateful for my help. I told him it was God who did it not me, he used me as His vessel to help him. I felt confident at this point especially after his mother arrived, he was not going to do anything to hurt himself. He promised me he would get the help offered to him. His mother was told to take him to the hospital for evaluation. The hospital was aware of this situation and was expecting him. On Saturday afternoon his mom called me and told me he was home and doing well. Sunday Mary and I went and picked him up and took him to church with us. He attended our Sunday school class and then worship afterwards. While in church I looked over at him and he was having trouble finding the passage our pastor was preaching from so I gave him my bible and took the church bible. The pastor was preaching about Jesus being the hope for our lives. I believe God was speaking directly to him. He had tears falling down his face but he was also smiling. After the service he tried to give me my bible back but I told him to keep it and read it. He was so grateful and told me thank you for saving his life and the bible. He gave Mary and I a big hug. I'm not sure but I think he accepted Christ that day. To God be the Glory.

Was this my purpose? No.....but its coming.

Lonna and I were getting along very well. She was now a christian and had accepted Jesus as her Lord and Savior. She knew I had done this some time back and it changed my life and she wanted to have the same thing. Not because I had it but because she needed it. We were talking about God and she said to me "I think God is punishing me" and I said "why would you think such a thing" and she said "well you know I have MS and He gave this to me because of all the bad things I did to you while we were married". Her MS was really hitting her hard lately and she was in and out of the hospital quite a bit with attacks. I was not sure how to respond to this but I told her God does not do those things. After we hung up I spoke to Mary about it and we both agreed I would need to speak to her more about this but not on the phone.

Proverbs 18:14 A mans spirit will endure sickness, but a crushed spirit who can bear?

A day of forgiveness

Lonna called me on September 14, 2002 and told me Julia just had a baby. She was in the Navy and had just got back from a deployment in the Mediterranean. I'm like WHAT! She said yes. It was a surprise for us all. I had seen her a month earlier and she did not look pregnant. Julia did not tell anyone she was pregnant and she said she did not even know until she went into labor and went to the hospital. A trip to Florida was now in order. I wanted to see my granddaughter. Her name was Emily. When we arrived Lonna was there. We greeted each other and were all sitting inside Julia's apartment when we began to talk about our lives now and some of the past. I told Lonna I wanted to talk to her about what she had told me about God punishing her. As we talked God's spirit began to move. I told her God does not punish us with sickness but will sometimes allow things to happen to get our attention. Lonna and I really never got along after our divorce and now I felt it was the time for forgiveness. I needed to forgive her for all the things she had done and ask for forgiveness for the things I had done. It was such a powerful time of forgiveness. The Holy Spirit filled the room, we could all feel Gods presence. We were able to forgive each other without reservation. We all cried and felt such a huge burden being lifted from our souls. I know God was pleased on this day. God is great. This was a very special time. Mary was so loving and compassionate to Lonna. I know Gods hands were all over this and nobody but Him could have done these things. Forgiveness and healing done in a flash. What a loving and mighty God we serve. Since this day of forgiveness Lonna has not had a single MS attack. Those used to put her in the hospital. Amen

Colossians 3:13 Bear with each other and forgive one another if any of you has a grievance against someone. Forgive as the Lord forgave you.

I found this quote online from The Bible Study Class web site about forgiveness:

"The pain of living with bitterness and unforgiveness can poison your soul and destroy you. When we forgive others, we are not saying what they did was Okay, but we are releasing them to God and letting go of it's hold on us"

John 4:14 But whoever drinks the water I give them will never thirst. Indeed, the water Igive them will become in them a spring of water welling up to eternal life.

God transforms us in many ways and in many forms. He is able to show us His love by us reading His word or through people we know. When Mary and I joined New Hope Baptist Church we immediately felt this is where we needed to be. Our pastor John Avant was great. He truly is a man of God. His sermons were passionate and from the word of God. He was a dynamic preacher and really kept the attention of those he was speaking to. I always felt like John was speaking directly to me when he preached which I liked. I felt God speaking to me on numerous occasions. We really liked New Hope. We plugged ourselves in by joining the choir. Talk about stepping out of your comfort zone. Mary loved to sing and was really good. Me on the other hand was not sure if I could sing but was willing to give it a try. We had met some people at IHop one morning where we would go almost every Saturday. We had seen them there several times before. The place was packed and they we waiting for a table. Mary and I were already seated at a table and we had room for them so we invited them to join us. They accepted. We found out during our visit they also went to New Hope and were in the choir. This is how we joined the choir. My first Sunday in the choir was the most scariest thing I think I have ever done. I was like a dear in headlights. All of those people in the congregation. It felt like they were all looking at me. The feeling went away pretty quick, I later found out the choir does the Living Christmas Tree every year and I was now part of the choir. Now remember when I said when I make a commitment I want to follow it through to the end...well now I am rethinking that. Not really but fear was in the air.

Psalm 100:2 Worship the Lord with gladness; come before Him with joyful songs.

Yippee I found my purpose......no way Jose'.

There was apprehension when we were practicing for the tree, not so much from Mary but mostly from me. I was not at all comfortable singing in front of a bunch of people let alone dancing with umbrellas. That's what we were going to do during this program. I have to admit as soon as we began the program I settled down and was able to do what I needed to do with no problems. It was like I was a pro with this all along. Gods hands were DEFINITELY in this one. The most amazing thing about doing this was hearing about all of the decisions that were being made as a result from people coming to the program. People were accepting Christ for the first time or they were re-dedicating their lives to Christ. What a blessing that was. There were plenty of Living Christmas Tree programs to follow. I finally got comfortable with it. Now I love it. Doing the program takes a lot of time and commitment but in the end it is all worth it. I am finding out Gods work can actually be fun.

In police work we would deal with situations which were mostly negative. I mean think about it, we write tickets, take people to jail, deal with domestic issues between husbands and wives, we would even give death notifications. Those were extremely hard to do. Sometimes though we would be involved in good things. I was responding to a person in labor call with EMS. I was really close to the location and so I arrived on scene first. When I went into the residence I found the lady who was in labor. She was in a recliner and was ready to have the baby. Now when I say ready to have the baby I mean ready to have the baby. The baby was crowning and I could see the top of the baby's head. I knew how to deliver a baby but never had up to this point so I told the person who was with her to bring me some clean towels and a pot of warm water. I got into position to deliver the baby when I heard a noise from behind me. When I looked it was the Paramedics coming in the door. I said thank you Jesus and turned this over to them. Jokingly I learned one thing

from this. NEVER GET ON A DELIVERY SCENE BEFORE THE
PARAMEDICS.

My purpose, Where art thou?...............Nice try.

There have been some tough times though that were trying
and hard to deal with. Not with family but with work, not with
citizens but with the Chief and my supervisors. Police work
can be very stressful and dealing with the public can be tiring.
We sometimes have to make decisions which may not be very
popular, especially when it comes to your boss. We did not
agree on a particular issue and we respectfully argued about
the decision I had made. I will not go into details about this
but the Chief was being unreasonable. I had followed policy
and procedures and the decision I made was the right one.
Most of the officers in the department felt the same way I did.
At this point I could do nothing right in his eyes. So I prayed. I
prayed God would give him restless nights and he and I would
come to an understanding. Later in the week the Chief had
came into the roll call room and was talking to our Major, I
heard him say he was not sleeping very well and was taking
the rest of the day off. Now I know prayer works.

Romans 12:12 Be joyful in hope, patient in affliction, faithful in prayer.

A faithful servant

God works out everything for you if you will let Him. There have been several times the world inside of me forgets He is there and I need to rely on Him for everything. It can be a challenge at times but at the end of the day we find out He does and will help us. Especially in times of despair, frustration or even uncertainty. There was an officer with our department who was having a lot of problems. I will keep his name confidential. He was drinking more than he should off duty and was going astray. He did not want to be around his family. Sound familiar. We spoke and prayed every day. I could tell he was struggling. We would often listen to christian music together in our patrol cars during our breaks. It was a great way for me to witness to him. We would read the words of the songs and compare them to what was going on in his life. I told him he really needed to get his priorities together and to sit down and speak with his wife about the issues and feelings he was having. He said he was not happy with his marriage but I could tell he was not sure about anything. I told him he was not happy because Satan has him right where he wanted him. He is putting doubt in your mind and will often say God can't or won't help you either. He puts you in situations that may feel good during the moment but afterwards the problems come back and they never go away. He loved his wife I could see it in his eyes when he spoke about her and he really loved his children. I was working one night and I got a call from dispatch to respond to the Police Department parking lot. The call was about an off duty officer who was involved in an accident and needed to speak with the on duty supervisor. When I arrived on scene the officer involved was the one I was counseling. He had been drinking and he looked like he had been in a fight. He told me he had been jumped by three guys when he left the bar he was at and he did not know where to turn to next so he came to see me. He was at his wits end. I called for an ambulance because he was pretty bad off and then afterwards I had to notify my supervisor of the incident. I knew when I called them this officer would be in some serious trouble and I could not do anything to stop what may happen to him. He was a great officer and I wanted him to succeed in every way. I prayed that our Chief would be merciful with him. He was suspended, not fired and afterwards he began to get help. I shared with him my situations before I found Jesus and I told him to trust in Jesus. After relying on God and trusting in Him to guide him down the right path he was able to turn his life and his marriage around. I am so proud of him for trusting in God. Trusting God was the only way of saving his marriage. Now his marriage is doing great. He is the Chief of Police for another agency and has been there for over ten years. I am so proud of him for staying the course. His whole life changed on the day he trusted God to take care of it. Isn't it what we all should be doing.......trusting God.

Psalm 46:1 God is our refuge and strength, an ever-present help in trouble.

Gods protection for all

I was working the midnight shift and I received a call to respond to a possible home invasion with the offender having a gun. I arrived on scene with my Lieutenant, he went around the back and I stayed in the front. My lieutenant made contact with the offender who was inside the residence. He was angry with his wife for cheating on him and he said was going to kill her and the man she was with. The other man was in the residence when the offender came in through a window on the rear of the residence. He told them he was going to kill them and the other man ran out through the front door, in his underwear I might add, and called the police. While my lieutenant spoke to him he would sometimes come to the front door where I was located. I could see he had a gun in his hand. I was worried he was going to come out and start shooting. Not only for my safety and the safety of the other officers but because I was the one he was going to face first and I did not want to shoot this man. As time went on I continued to pray this incident would end without anyone getting hurt. The stand off lasted about an hour when our K-9 officer showed up. He went around the side of the house with his dog. His dogs name was Beau. Beau liked to bark but he was really barking a lot on this night. My lieutenant told our offender if he did not come out with his hands up we were going to send in the dog. Within a few minutes the offender came out the front door. He had his hands up and when I told him to get on the ground he did with no hesitation. I placed him in hand cuffs and put him in my patrol car. I asked him why did he give up and he said he didn't want to get bit by the dog. WOW he would rather me shoot him than get bit by a dog. God helped all of us on this day

Romans 10:17 So faith comes from hearing, and hearing through the word of God.

Surely my purpose is here now. Who are you kidding...and stop calling me Shirley.

God works through us in so many different ways. He does it by us talking with our friends, Sunday School classes, Choir and so many others. Missions is a great way to do Gods work. It gives you a chance to help others come to know Christ. One day while I was working I received a phone call from Hugh Kirby a minister from our church. He told me he needed my help. Well of course I said Okay. He said he needed me to play golf for him and I said Okay just tell me when and where. He said the when is in April and the where is in Thailand. I said did you say Thailand? He laughed and said yes. The church would like you to go to Thailand and help teach golf at a college there. I was a Semi Pro golfer who played on the amature circuit in Atlanta. I was not sure if I would be able to get the time off to go. I looked at my schedule and spoke to my supervisor and I was able to get the time off to go. So in April myself and three others, Steve, Wendell, and Ted flew to Thailand. Twenty one hours to Korea then another eight hours to Bangkok and then the next morning another five hours to Chiang Mai. I was exhausted and we haven't even started yet. We stayed in Chiang Mai for three days and did a couple of golf clinics there. I was not feeling well and was actually not able to eat much. My room mate and I started to pray for healing and the words "stop taking your malaria tablets" came to mind. We were all taking them because we were going to go to Laos for a day. I was told we would not be going and so I could stop taking them. The next morning I am feeling much better and was able to eat with no more problems. We then took a six hour van ride to Lampang where we stayed for another four days. We were doing golf clinics all day long. Some of them were six to eight hours long. We also went to Yonok College there in Lampang. The students there were awesome. Some could speak broken English and others could not at all. We had a translator and she did very well. One night we took the student to Pizza Hut. They were so funny. Some had never eaten pizza before and was unsure about even trying it, but once they did they enjoyed it. What teenager doesn't like pizza. They were your typical young adults who was as interested in us as we were with them. We would tell corny jokes and some we even had to be explained. Trying to explain it was funnier than the joke. We even had to show them how Americans eat pizza. What a great time we had. On the last day we were at the college the students wanted to serve us dinner. A traditional Thai dinner. They set up the tables around the pool area on campus and hung lights and dressed up the tables. They were so excited about doing this for us. They were gracious hosts. Before we ate our dinner a prayer was said in English by Mike the director of Asian Sports Academy and then, Dr. Nurun the president of the college, who was also christian said one in Thai. When he started his prayer I began to weep. I was not sure why but I knew God was speaking to me. I heard Him say this was all about Him and not me and He was reminding me of this. It was so clear to me. It took me a few minutes to get my composure. Steve even asked me if I was Okay and I said yes I'll be fine. This was again another slap on the back of my head. I was so caught up in the moment I had forgotten why I was even there. We sometimes forget what we do is for Gods glory not ours. I shared this time I had with God with every one there and we prayed about how God was so good. Some of the students there did not know Christ and after we had left Mike told us the students began to ask a lot of questions. AMEN. Oh and the food...it was great!

Mark 16:15 He said to them, "go into the world and preach the gospel to all creation"

I still don't see my purpose.....You are looking in all the wrong places!

I love it when God speaks to me. I am still learning how to recognize His voice and pay attention to it. I want to make sure its Him and not me. One day in September I was in a training class. I was learning how to write search warrants and affidavits. My lieutenant was in the class with me. I started to think about the School Resource Officers position at Fayette County High School. My thoughts were to put in for the position. I was not sure if the position was even available. I asked my Lieutenant was there an opening and he said he didn't think so. I told him I was thinking about it and was interested in the position if it became available. He told me to write a letter of interest and turn it in. So after the class I wrote my letter of interest and turned it in. I quickly got a response from the Chief. It was a one sentence letter. There are no openings for this position. Not very formal I thought. Well in November the officer who was holding the position came to me and said "I hear you are interested in coming over to the school". I told him only if the position was available. He said he was wanting to come out and this year was going to be his last year. I asked him to let me know when he was going to submit his request to come out and then I would resubmit my letter of interest again. He said Okay. In January the following year he submitted his letter asking to come out of the school. Immediately the Chief put out a notice to the department saying that the SRO position was available and for anyone who was interested to put in their letter of interest. I submitted my letter. This Chief and I did not get along and my feeling was I would not get the position. As it turns out not one officer put in for the position. The Chief at this point had to give me the position. I could tell he wasn't happy in fact he had the Major call me in and tell me I got the position. He tried to make it sound like I would not like it by saying "now you know you have to do this for a minimum of three years" and "this is a weekend and holidays off job with no over time". I'm like where is the down side to this. Gods will be done.

Galatians 6:9 Let us not become weary in doing good, for at the proper time we will reap a harvest if we do not give up.

The Chief was constantly on me for one thing or another. I was always in the spot light with him. The Chief called for a department meeting one day and the entire department was there. The meeting was for him explain to us why another officer was terminated. There were rumors and speculations going around the department about this issue and so he wanted to give us his position about it. The City manager was also in attendance. As the meeting progressed a lot of questions were being asked and no real answers were given. To be frank, the officers were afraid to ask questions because of possible retaliation from the Chief and the Major. Both of them were like two peas in a pod. The Chief said he was done with the meeting and there were still questions being answered by the City Manager. The Major kept interrupting him and would answer the questions being asked and so the officers would not ask any more questions. One officer finally stood up and said to the City Manager, if you want us to talk you will have to ask the Major to leave the room. So he asked him to leave the room. He was not happy at all. Then all of the officers started telling how the two of them ran the department. Usually by fear and intimidation and we no longer want them as our Chief and Major. The entire department did a unanimous vote of no confidence for both of them. Two weeks later both of them resigned from the department. We were all glad they were gone. Now the department had an opportunity to heal and we started to trust each other again. Things were going well in the department and at the school. I was settling in and getting use to the students. God was working and giving me opportunities I did not expect. Students were asking me to pray with them. At times I was overwhelmed with emotion thinking about how the students trusted me to pray with them. What an honor it was for me. I can remember a time when I would not even say a prayer at dinner time with my family and now I am praying with these kids. WOW!

Ephesians 6:18 And pray in the spirit on all occasions with all kinds of prayer requests. With this in mind, be alert and always keep on praying for all the Lords people.

This has to be my purpose now......no way dude!

A hatchet buried

My Mom and Dad lived in Lexington Kentucky and my father was beginning to have issues with his driving and forgetting where he was going. He actually drove up onto a curb one time and my mom asked him why he did that and he said he didn't know. Then his health began to deteriorate and the doctors found out he had a bad heart valve and he needed a bypass. He had to have major heart surgery. The physicians replaced one of his heart valves and did a bypass on two others. It seemed like he was in surgery for a long time. The doctors said it was touch and go for awhile. Afterwards he was sent to a rehab center for his rehab and recovery. On one occasion I had gone up to Lexington to visit with him and mom. My dad looked great. He was talking with us and having good conversations without him having trouble finding his words. I don't know why but he loved shark week and it was that week. He asked me if I had seen any sharks when I went scuba diving. All in all it was a great week. Mom said he has not had a week like that in a while. I had gone up on Monday and I had to come back to Atlanta on Friday, so around lunch time, I told dad I had to leave to go home and he said Okay. When I got up to leave he put his hand out to shake it and I said can I give you a hug instead of the hand shake. Now I will say this, my dad was not a hugger. I wanted to give him a hug but I was not sure of what he might say. He would shake your hand but no hugs, but he said yes to a hug. I got a big hug from him. I was surprised but very happy he said yes. I told him I loved him and he said I love you too and I went back to Atlanta. I will say, I don't ever remember my dad telling me he loved me. That was how he was, he didn't show a lot of emotion when it came to those things. It wasn't a bad thing we all knew he loved us. On Sunday evening mom called and told me dad had passed away. He had a seizure and did not recover from it. I believe that week was the calm before the storm. My last memory of my father was a hug and an I love you. I am so grateful for that memory. I will hold that in my heart forever.

Another God story

Once there was a time when my church asked me to write a God story. They wanted to use them for the Prime Time news letter. The Prime Time Ministry is for the older adults in our church. So I decided to write one on how I got the resource officer position at the high school. Afterwards I turned it in and never really thought about it again. About a year or so went by and I got a phone call from the new Chief asking me if could come and speak with him. I went to the department and he had asked me would I be interested in a promotion to lieutenant. He said I would have to come out of the school if I got the promotion. There was an opening and I was on the promotion roster. He told me to think about it and to let him know as soon as possible. I spoke to my wife about it and I also prayed about it. I decided to take the promotion if it was offered to me. About a week later the Chief calls me and tells me I did not give get the promotion and he gave it to another officer. I was a bit disappointed but I was not really asking to leave the school. Then two months later another position became available and this time I was not asked. I was a little put out over this because I was still on the promotion roster and was actually more qualified than the other officers and now I am upset about the whole thing. Especially not even being considered. I called and made an appointment to speak with the Chief. The next day I met with the Chief and I asked him why I was not considered for the last opening for lieutenant. He told me he did not think I really wanted to leave the school. I said I probably didn't want to but it would have been nice to at least be considered. I was respectful but I was still upset. Afterwards I called to vent to my wife and she listened. She is very good at that and does not try and fix things. Later she called me back and asked me if I had seen our emails at home, I said no and she said go to our emails and look at the Prime Time one and then call me back afterwards. So I went to our emails and opened the Prime Time news letter and low and behold the letter I wrote was the one posted for the week. Remember this letter was written about how I got my position at the school almost a year earlier. Okay lord I hear ya! I called my wife back and she was kinda laughing about the situation and I said "I cant even be mad anymore" my wife loves it when I get the proverbial Anthony DiNozzo slap on the back of the head. I hate it when He does that to me. I think that's where my bald spot is coming from. I take it my work here at the school was not done yet?

John 4:34 Jesus said to them, "My food is to do the will of Him who sent me and to accomplish His work.

Times were really good. The department had settled down and I was finally in the groove at the school. My time at the school was awesome. I was teaching classes and going to the Prom. They don't do Proms like I remembered anymore. I thought you danced face to face, Oh well. A bunch of Graduations are now behind me. There were some students I didn't think would graduate but did. I can't help but be proud of them for their hard work. I was given several opportunities to witness and pray with the students. They would come to my office and tell me how a friend or a family member would be involved in an accident or was sick and they would ask me to pray with them. Not too many officers can say they had chances like that. What an honor it was for me to even be asked to do that with these children. I believe that the students saw my heart and trusted me enough to come and ask.

Ephesians 6:18 And pray in the Spirit on all occasions with all kinds of prayers and requests. With this in mind, be alert and always keep on praying for all the Lords people.

When I turned 55 years old the City manager called me and said the city wanted to offer me an early retirement package. I had spoken to the Chief earlier about the rumors of the early retirement offers and I knew I would probably be one of many they were going to offer it to. I told him I could not afford to retire completely and he told me he would have to fill the SRO position sooner or later and he preferred to fill it with someone who had experience. I still was not sure I wanted to retire but I said I would look at it. So I went to our meeting and the package was pretty good. My wife was with me at the meeting and when we got in the car she told me the offer was too good to pass up.

So I accepted the package and took retirement. Now I am unemployed. I have not had that feeling for over thirty years and I have to admit it was a bit scary. I had to completely separate from the department for thirty days but after a couple of weeks the Chief called me and told me he was having a problem filling the position. He asked me if I wanted to come back as a part time officer and I could work a teachers schedule. This qualified me to continue drawing my retirement pay. I told him I would come back. So now Gods work continues.

Philippians 1:6 And I am sure of this, that He who began a good work in you will bring it to completion at the day of Jesus Christ.

As it turns out the Chief was also offered retirement. He actually retired after I came back to work part time. For the next five years I continued to worked at school. There were several things I had to deal with but I think the students had a general respect for me.

Some may not have liked the police part but they liked and respected me as a person. I tried my best to listen to their complaints and concerns and I always tried to treat them all the same. I had one of our star basketball players come to me after church one Sunday. He attended the same church I did. He said that he had been looking for me and he had been designated the spokesperson for the team. He told me the team had got together and was talking about me. He said with the way things were going these days with the country being so divided, racism and violence towards the police they wanted me to know they were happy I was their resource officer. He said they all agreed I was not racist and I treated everyone fairly and they all wanted to say thank you. Once I had time to really think about what he had told me I could not help but feel a bit over whelmed. I was not concerned about who they were, what color they were or what they did at the school. They were kids and needed to be treated as such. All to often we say "Why cant you make good decisions" or "cant you see this". Well they can't because they can't. Their brain is not developed enough yet. It doesn't work that way. I believe God gave me the opportunity to be around these kids because I had a different outlook on them. Yes I was the police and I know sometimes I had a job to do but I never let my emotions drive my train, especially when it came to the kids, I was always fair and honest with them. I had a good working relationship with the faculty and staff and we always tried to work as a team. We would make our decisions on a case by case basis because locking up a child is not always the best thing for the child.

Proverbs 13:24 Who ever spares the rod hates their children, but the one who loves their children is careful to discipline them.

An opportunity to witness

My opportunity to pray at the school was awesome. There was a time however when I was told not to pray. The head football coach and I started a tradition where we would meet on the thirty yard line at the beginning of a game and pray. It would only be the two of us. We would pray for the safety of the players, coaches and officials. Plus a special prayer for those in attendance. The prayer would last about a minute at best but on Monday following a Friday night game I was called to the principles office and was told that I was no longer allowed to pray before the games. He told me that we could not pray in front of the students. I asked him did someone complain and he said no but he was trying to avoid a complaint. I was not very happy with that so I went to the football coach and told him what had happened. We both were upset about it. We decided to pray about it and see what

God has to say. Later that week we decided to have our prayer but instead of it being on the field we would meet in front of the field house. No students were around and we felt this would be Okay. This was perfect because now instead of it being the coach and I, it is now with all of the coaches, Police Officers and EMS personnel. We went from two praying to at least ten. God is so good.

Okay show me my purpose!!............patience Padawon, patience.

My time at the Police Department ended in May of 2017. I took a second retirement and after 28 years I was now out of Law Enforcement. The city asked me if I wanted to take a part time job working in Code Enforcement. I was not sure about the job or what I was going to do but I was Okay with working a part time job so I said Okay.

Off again on missions

Before I started working in Code Enforcement I was able to go on another missions trip. This time to Wales. New Hope was taking the Gospel choir and was doing concerts around the local areas in Wales. The church had been doing this for about 15 years before I went. It was so much fun but exhausting at the same time. I was on the connect team and our job was to go the venue where we would be performing that night and hand out fliers for the concert. I was a bit skeptical at first about knocking on doors but we were told at the residences there would be a sticker on the door if they did not want anyone to solicit anything to them. When we would make contact with the residence we would tell them who we were and about the concert. Most were very receptive but some were not. The team consisted of eight people and we would split up into two teams. We were in the village of Aberfan and was going to do a concert there that night. We were handing out fliers when we knocked on a door and an elderly couple answered. They were probably in their 80's. I told them why we were there and they invited us in for a short visit. They were so sweet. They showed us all of the family photos and they even told us a story about how his wife received a gift from the Queen after she had turned 80 years old. She was very proud of that for sure. He asked me if I knew the story of what had happened there fifty years ago. I told him yes. Here is the story. In 1966 the village of Aberfan lost an entire generation of children including 28 adults when a mountain of rock and shale slid down covering the village in a matter of minutes. You could still see the sorrow in the faces of those who remembered. He said it was a tragedy for sure. The gentleman I was speaking with said he helped dig the survivors out and then helped with the recovery of the children. I could tell it still bothered him. We stayed for a little while and we invited them to come to the concert and went on our way. I bet I walked more than 12,000 steps each day. We would sing at local churches and would pack the house. I will say the Welsh people love to sing gospel music. What an experience it was and to see so many people coming to know the Lord. This trip changed my life in many ways. I have grown to appreciate the things I have and to not worry about the things I don't. What a blessing. I had a special time during this trip with my pastor Rhys Stenner. We were stopped at a scenic view after one of our concerts and he was telling me about the area we were in and the history behind it. We spoke for a few more minutes and then he asked me if I wanted to ride with him. Well of course I said yes. Its not very often when you are able to have some quality time with your pastor. Rhys is a great pastor. He is very passionate about his relationship with our Lord and there is no doubt at all that he loves his calling to preach. My car ride with him was awesome. It may seem insignificant to some but for me I enjoyed our 40 minute ride. We just talked about things going on in our lives and the mission trip and before I knew it the ride was over. It was a very special time for me to spend with my pastor.

I do not like to paint

I came back to a new adventure after the mission trip. Code Enforcement. It was nice to have a different job but as time went on I was not very happy with it. The job was like watching paint dry. Not much to do and very political. I am not a politician and did not like playing the game of favoritism. I tried to stay away from all of that. I was grateful to have the job but I was not happy and after about a year and a half in code enforcement I was starting to think about possibly looking for something else. I prayed about my situation and asked God to show me what His will would be for me. I spoke to Mary about how I was feeling and told her I felt God was wanting me to work in or around a Christian environment. I was not really sure what that meant. Surely He did not want me to be a preacher. Mary said laughing no I don't think so. But I felt pretty strong about this message I was getting. I was at home one night and was looking at

Facebook and I saw a message to me from a teacher and coach I knew from Fayette County High School. He told me Landmark Christian School in Peachtree City was looking for a security officer and asked me would I be interested in the job. I never looked at messenger before and I was not even sure how to open it. Mary had to show me how. I was interested in hearing the offer so I told him yes. A few days later the director of security for the school contacted me and we spoke on the phone for about 20 minutes. He had asked me what I was looking for and he said Okay he would get back with me later the following week. I felt good about the conversation but was not sure about him. I went home that night and prayed about it asking God if this was in His will to please leave the door open. He contacted me the following week and he was able to give me what I asked for and offered me the position. He wanted me to start right away so I gave my notice to the city and started with the school the next week. God is so good!

1 John 5:14 This is the confidence we have in approaching God: that if we ask anything according to His will, He hears us.

Getting this job was a blessing. To be at a Christian school and work with kids again is what I believe God wants me to do. The school is Pre-K to 4th grade which is something I was not used to but I was able to adjust rather quickly. The faculty and staff is amazing and fun to work with. The students are awesome. To hear those children sing on Chapel days will make you cry. A pure heart for the Love of Christ is amazing to watch. Their spirits are filled with laughter and joy. Innocence in its truest form. WOW.

Matthew 21:16 "Do you hear what these children are saying?" they ask Him. "Yes" replied Jesus, "have you never read, "from the lips of children and infants you, Lord, have called forth your praise.

W.W.J.D.

I truly believe we need to fall back on the What Would Jesus Do (W.W.J.D.) principle. God never wants us to fail but we often do. We should learn from our failures but sometimes we don't. We are sinners and we will always fall short of His glory. When we fall short with our kids though we often pay the price and so do they. When I worked at the High School I would deal with kids who were being raised by a single mom or dad or by their grandparents. I believe the absence of the father in a home is one of the biggest problems we face today. Kids need to have their dad in their lives, even daughters. Dads teach their kids how to be respectful to each other. To teach the simple things to their sons like opening a door for a lady. When their daughters see their dad do these things they learn this is the way they should be treated. It is the simple things that make the biggest difference. The yes Ma'ams and yes Sirs work wonders for them as well.

We should teach our children to respect themselves then each other. We should always praise them when they do well. We should recognize their failures also but with constructive criticism and to not belittle them into feeling like they don't matter. They do matter and even when we criticize them, if done right, they will appreciate it in the end. Believe it or not Kids want to be disciplined. I had a student one time tell me the reason why he misbehaves is because its the only time his father talks to him. This goes to the old adage that any attention is better than none. So Sad. I truly believe that behavior is learned and it usually comes from whoever is raising them. I would ask myself all the time why does this child behave like this and then I meet the parents and it explains it all.

Proverbs 22:6 Start children off on the way they should go, and even when they are old they will not turn from it.

A red phone to Jesus

We all remember the DC sniper incident in October of 2002, during that time I was at choir practice when John Conrad our choir director stopped and said he felt the need to pray. Afterwards John said he had a vision of a moose and did that have any significance to anyone. Well at the time no one said anything so we continued with our practice. A few days later I was watching the news and the FBI had introduce the official in charge of the sniper case. He was answering some questions. His name was Charles Moose. I was very surprised to see this and I know John would want to know. At the next choir practice I told John about it and he was shocked and then said he felt a need for a special prayer for him and his team. Later that night the DC snipers was apprehended. John has a special ability to hear God speaking to him. We often say he has a red phone to God. Actually he has learned to listen and pay attention to when God was speaking to him. Following Gods purpose is as simple as that. Listening! Then doing. That's the hard part. Some are afraid of what others may think, others may feel embarrassed or not worthy to even pray for others needs. I tell you I felt the same way. I was too shy to even say a prayer in front of my kids at a meal. I would fall apart if some one would ask me to say a prayer in front of our Sunday school class, or speak about the bible like I was a scholar. I can tell you I don't know the bible like others do but I am learning every day. This is another way of following Christ. When the apostles were asked by Jesus to follow Him. Did they say oh whatever, no...they got up and followed Him. The more we follow the more we can lead.

Matthew 4:19 Come follow me and I will send you to fish for people. Matthew 20:26 Not so with you, instead, whoever wants to become great among you must be your servant

We are given the choice to follow Jesus. We do this through our faith. Believing what He is saying and offering to us, Eternal Life. Eternal life...who doesn't want that. I myself believe He is our Savior and I will spend eternity with Him one day. I didn't receive a letter in the mail, an email or a tweet from Him. Only the assuring words in the bible telling me so. I surrendered myself to His teachings and am trying to pattern and live my life like His. I am not perfect in any way and I am a sinner like everyone else. But doing good works or being a good person is not enough. Our relationship with Him should be above our own will and desires. I like the idea that once I decided to follow Christ I then became a disciple. Not that I am worthy of this title but in reality a disciple is what we all are once we begin to follow Christ.

We want to see things before we believe in them. I'll believe it when I see it, well if this was the case then what good would having faith be. As a follower of Jesus Christ there will be times of struggle. We often think now with God in our lives things won't happen to us anymore. This is not true. Having Christ in our lives makes things easier to cope with when they do happen. In fact the burden of sorrow helps our relationship with Christ grow. It brings us closer to Him and strengthens our relationship. I have watched miracles happen during times of sorrow and despair. I didn't see it then but I do now. We see Gods mercy and grace only when we need them the most. We don't pay attention to it when we think we don't need it. Going through trials in our lives is what makes us stronger. We should be thanking God for everything in our lives good and bad. Praising God is an act of faith during these times and helps you grow in your faith. Jesus guides us, comforts us, and binds us together during the worst times in our lives. Our trust and faith in Him is what will sustain our relationship. When there is a time in your life when you think your faith is fading or even gone, then go to the scriptures and start reading. Gods words are some of the most comforting and reassuring words you will ever find. I found this to be true when I became a christian and felt alone. With my family falling apart and no where to turn Gods grace and mercy helped me through it. Gods strength is yours too. He can and will help you through any trial you may be facing. I for one like happy endings. Don't you? Finding faith in a world which seems to be falling apart is pretty exhausting. We look here and there and everywhere and we never seem to find what it is we are looking for. Do we even know what it is we want? The problem is we are placing our faith in the wrong person. Trusting man to take care of things he can't possibly do only complicates things. All too often we get it wrong and sometimes it turns out worse. I'm not saying we don't sometimes get it right, what I'm saying is having faith in Jesus is the best way to fight the demons inside you. Having faith in Jesus Christ is entirely different. We completely trust Him and take God at His word no mater what. Or do we? Every time something goes wrong in our lives or when we fail we forget God is there. He has and always will be there. As humans we sometimes fail to ask for Gods help, but if the situation we face is bad enough we will forget He's there and we will want to fix it without His help. We want immediate results. Well I have news for you! Gods timing is not on our time schedule. Without Gods grace, we expect way too much in a short period of time. This is where we fall short and fail. Sometimes God wants us to feel the pain of the situation we are in, but He also reminds us He is always with us. Remember the poem "Footprints in the sand" where in the end the Lord was asked "Why when I needed you most, you have not been there for me?" the Lord replied "The years when you have seen only one set of footprints, my child, is when I carried you". We sometimes want instant results but forget the journey is part of the results. I believe if it wasn't for my journey my end result would not have been salvation. I shudder to think what my life would be like if it wasn't for my salvation. The beautiful thing is, Jesus was with me every step of the way, even though I didn't think so. Even when I didn't know Jesus and I look back I can see signs He was trying to reach me. I remember a time when I was over seas in the military I was approach by one of the guys I worked with. He wanted me to go to church with him. He was reaching out to me because he knew me and saw the things I was doing and going through. I was not paying attention and was ignoring Gods servant trying to do His will. I was too stubborn to realize it. I thought I could fix it on my own. I know how that turned out. Lonna and I speak every now and then and we often say and wonder how things might have been if we had known Christ earlier. What would our lives look like now. I believe Gods will was done. Mary and I love each other very much and I can't see my life without her. God sent an angel to me the day I met Mary and I will be forever in His debt for it. Now that was crazy. I am in His debt forever and I can never repay what He has done for me. Lonna and I went through some very hard times and it wasn't until we came to know Jesus as our Lord and Savior that things began to change. I believe Gods will was done for both of us. I know my faith is stronger than ever and nothing will ever change my belief that Jesus Christ is Lord.

Getting to know Him

God wants us to know Him better and one way we can do that is to read His word. Often times we find or say we don't have the time or don't want to. We need to change this way of thinking. Gods word is what helped me through the difficult times in my life as well as the good times. For every situation you may be facing I can tell you there is an answer for it in the word of God. Trust me I know. You have to believe the words you are reading and they are Gods words not ours.

2 Timothy 3:16 All Scripture is God-breathed and is useful for teaching, rebuking, correcting and training in righteousness

Acts 2:47 Praising God and enjoying the favor of all the people. And the Lord added to their number daily those who were being saved.

Prayer is the greatest way to speak with God. The nice thing about prayer is you can talk to Him anytime and anywhere you want. You can talk about anything too. It took me a while to learn how to pray. Here is my secret. Talk to Him like you would talk to anyone else. It does not have to be all theatrical like you were a graduate from the seminary. Just talk. I knew a man who started his prayers with "Whats up God its me again". When I first heard him say that I laughed but quickly found out this was how he prayed. I learned an awful lot from his prayers and the way he prayed.

Proverbs 3:6 Listen for Gods voice in everything you do, everywhere you go; He's the one who will keep you on track.

Take time to listen. It requires a listening heart. Its hard to listen when its noisy so find a good place to go where its quiet. Remove yourself from distractions. I read somewhere where the author said something like "God wants to feed us and we must learn to sit quietly while He serves us a banquet for our souls" Its not easy but you can do it. I think it requires patience. Really I have a lot of patience! NOT! I do love it when God speaks to me. Sometimes its a quiet voice and other times its like being run over by a bus. I remember one time I was mad at the world, or at least it seemed that way, anyway it was during the time when my church was doing the Living Christmas Tree. I said I was only going to do the tree part of the program and nothing else. Through out the week that's what I did. Wouldn't you know it, I felt uncomfortable all week. On Saturday night I had decided to sit with Mary after I was done with my part and watch the rest of the program with her. When I sat down next to her I was not able to sit still. Mary told me to stop fidgeting and moving around so much. I could hear God clearly saying "This is not about you its about me, you should be up there finishing the program"! WOW talk about clear as a bell. Oh no, here comes another Anthony DiNozzo slap to the back of my head again. He has done that to me a few times. I don't think it will be my last either. I told God from now on as long as I was able I would do the entire program. I was able to settle down after that. I did the entire program on Sunday. I hope God was pleased. I am still learning to listen and I'm sure I will meet Jesus before I completely figure it out. I did however figure out one thing, its hard to hear Him when your mouth is moving, so stop talking and take time to listen.

Psalm 147:11 "The Lord delights in those who fear Him, who put their hope in His unfailing love."

Rejecting God or simply disobeying Him can be destructive and dangerous. God has ways of disciplining us if we disobey Him. Moses had trouble when he delivered the Israelite's from their torment. God showed them many miracles while they were going to the promised land but they still did not truly believe. They were inpatient and could not wait for Gods plan to work. They began to doubt God even existed. They began calling Moses a liar. They formed a golden calf as their own god and worshiped it. God was not Happy and punished them. Many died. They were made to wonder the wilderness for 40 years until all who sinned against Him were gone. We need to pay attention when God speaks to us. We will hear God tell us things He wants us to do but then we say no way I'm not doing that. Why? Because its inconvenient or I can't afford it. When God called me to go to Wales in 2017 on a mission trip I was not sure if I had the money to go. So instead of not going I committed to going and God provided the money for me. Not only did He provide it but He provided it all. God pleaded with the Israelite's asking them to listen to Him.

Psalm 81:8-14 Hear me, my people, and I will warn you—if you would only listen to me, Israel. You shall have no foreign god among you: you shall not worship any god other than me. I am the Lord your God, who brought you up out of Egypt. Open wide your mouth and I will fill it. But my people would not listen to me: Israel would not submit to me. So I gave them over to their stubborn hearts to follow their own devices. If only my people would listen to me, if Israel would only follow my ways, how quickly I would subdue their enemies and turn my hand against their foes.

When I was born I can't say what my mom was thinking. I was having so much trouble trying to survive. Did she say he's being a burden right now and he's not even a week old, or, is he going to be a problem for me in the future, or, did she say let him go. No she prayed for me and wanted me to survive, to live. She never gave up on me. In 2018 the Governor of New York, Andrew Cuomo, signed into law a bill allowing mothers to abort their children even at the time of their births and after. A child could be murdered directly after birth if the parent and doctors allowed it. In New York a person was charged with the murder of his pregnant wife and abortion for his unborn baby. She was eight months pregnant and now he is only facing charges of murder. The new law caused the state of New York to vacate the abortion charge and so now he faces no consequences for the murder of the unborn baby. The state of Virginia followed suit and the Governor there, Ralph Northam, also wanted to pass a law following the same model of New York's. If these laws were in existence in 1957 my mother could of let me die and it would have been Okay. No consequences! These doctors took an oath to preserve life not to take it. Hypocrites in it truest form. It is not my place to judge, that's Gods job. This issue is so disturbing to me and If this does not bother you then all I can say is I'll be praying for you. Gods gifts should not be mistreated or taken lightly. God calls children a blessing and a gift to all of us. These people who allow the taking of an innocent life should be held accountable and at the time of their judgment they should be made to look at those innocent faces for eternity. Nothing is worse than going to hell for eternity but this would be very close to that. Our time here on earth is limited and we have to make the best of it while we are on it. We can be in the world but should not be of the world. I wish I had paid attention when people were trying to reach me and tell me about Jesus. God has a plan for all of us. We don't know what it is, only He knows. I can say Gods plan is better than any plan we have. I want to make one point here. Lets say for argument sake I am right in my belief, would you rather live your life for Christ and change your ways for the better and know you will go to heaven for eternity or would you want to live your life doing the same old thing and getting the same old results and not have anything to look forward too. If I am right then when you die without Christ you will live in turmoil forever in THE OTHER PLACE. If you change your life for the better than even if I am wrong your life would still have some meaning. Now let me say this, I know I am **NOT** wrong. I have seen and experienced too many things for me to be wrong. I know because the bible tells me so. It is so easy to forget about God when we are faced with difficult or uncertain times. Our faith can falter or even be tested. We can sometimes have doubts He exists. Satan likes to put junk in our heads. Tell Satan to go away, he is not wanted, in Jesus name, and he will run. Saying the name Jesus to him makes him burn even more. God knows we are going to struggle and fail at times. Struggles comes in many shapes and sizes, persecution, worry, fear just to name a few. We tend to depend on ourselves to take care of those struggles and not on God. Struggling can take over your life and your thoughts if you don't handle them in the right way. We should not lose site of what God can do for us and we should never give up or lose hope. He has given us plenty of assurances with His words in the bible.

1 Thessalonians 2:13 And we also thank God continually because, when receive the word of God, which you heard from us, you accepted it not as human word, but as it actually is, the word of God, which is indeed at work in you who believe.

1 Timothy 4:10 That is why we labor and strive, because we have put our hope in the

living God, who is the Savior of all people, and especially of those who believe.

John 20:27 Then He said to Thomas, "Put your finger here: see my hands. Reach out and put it into my side. Stop doubting and believe.

Matthew 5:39 I tell you, do not resist an evil person. If anyone slaps you on the right cheek, turn to them the other cheek also.

The situations Christians face these days can be very frustrating and frankly, sometimes will make you angry. I see our faith being attacked almost daily now. It started with removing Jesus from our public schools and now crosses are being torn down, wanting to remove "In God We Trust" from our currency, or prayer not allowed after a football game just because someone thinks its offensive. They use the excuse of the separation of church and state as a reason to complain. Government officials cave in because it would either cost too much to fight in court or they don't want the negative publicity. Well we as Christians need to stand up and say this behavior is no longer acceptable. We have the first amendment on our side and we have the right to say enough is enough. A minority should never rule the majority. I am sure there are more Christians than atheists. Okay enough with the politics. I told y'all I was not a politician. You know what.........WE NEED REVIVAL!

Psalm 85:6 Will you not revive us again, that your people may rejoice in you?

Sin

Lets talk about sin for just a minute. It comes in so many different forms. Your words, deeds, actions and beliefs can all be sinful. We often see sin right in front of us and do nothing about it. It is all around us. Then we cry about it and still do nothing to stop it. We are all sinners and we fall short of the glory of God.

Romans 3:23 For all have sinned and fall short of the glory of God.

When we sin I see a picture of God frowning with disappointed. He knows we can do better and He wants us to rely on Him and not of ourselves. When we don't put Him first then we try and do things without Him, this is when we sin. We know that sin can take over our lives. Pride, greed, pornography, adultery, excessive drinking, using the Lords name in vain are just a few. Satan enjoys it when we have these issues in our lives. Why? Because he knows when we are in sin then we are not with God. But when we are with God then Satan can't take hold of our lives. Satan wants to destroy all of Gods children and seeks us out at our most vulnerable times. Satan wants us to be miserable and when we don't trust in God to help us then he wins. Don't give in to temptations you know are against Gods will for us. Satan has a one track mind and wants us to fail at every turn. He wants us to be still and quiet and not worship God. I will say this, Satan is never still or quiet. He will work on you until you give in to him. He does not give up. He will put things in your mind that can make sense. He will use simple excuses such as "you don't have to go to church to worship God" or "I really don't like organized religion". A bit lame if you ask me and besides we know that's not true because the bible says God wants us in His house to worship Him. God wants us to live out our faith among the people and not alone. We certainly can't bring others to Christ when we are alone. I believed in this lie for over a year and was not going to church. Satan had me believing that his way was the only way and I was not going to go to a church that did not see or believe in what I wanted. Do you see the wrong word here? Boy was I wrong. Finally I listen to God and I am now attending church regularly and loving every minute of it. A renewed spirit. Satan will sometimes use other Christians around you to poison your mind into thinking the wrong things. Kinda sounds like the serpent with Eve. Sin is sin. We can't put lipstick on a pig. Forgiveness of sin is also forgiveness. Once you are forgiven it is washed in the blood of Jesus and never to be seen again. I sometimes see myself asking God to forgive me for a sin that He had forgiven me of years ago and He says what sin. Once forgiven always forgiven. It doesn't matter what you have done. Gods grace and mercy is always enough. We are washed in the blood and are as white as snow! THE GREAT ASSURANCE!

Psalm 150:1 Praise the Lord! Praise God in His sanctuary; praise Him in His mighty heavens.

Are you faithful, we know God is, if so then your life will be filled with more joy and rewards than your bucket can ever hold. Don t let others or situations rob you of your joy or your chance to truly change. I could actually use the word transformed. I hope this book shows you it does not matter what has happened in your life, or the things you have done. Just believe there is hope through the grace and mercy of Jesus Christ. I know for a fact God changed my life in such a dramatic way. People who knew me before I knew Christ say I am not the same person. They are right, I am not the same person. God changed me forever. I can't even imagine my life without Christ in it. The people He has put in my life and the things I have been able to accomplish for Him, because of Him, has simply been beautiful and amazing. I love doing Gods work. Its not hard for me to follow Him. He has helped me in ways I can never repay and I don't think He wants me to. He wants me to stay in His will and lead others to Him. Am I perfect? No! Will I ever be perfect? No! But Christ is and He always will be. Following Christ is first and foremost in my home for both Mary and I. We do our best to find His will and then follow the path He has laid down for us. If its not Him speaking to us we will normally find out pretty quick. If it is Him then we know He is pleased, especially when we follow Him and do what He wants us to do. Are you needing something? Do you feel empty or feel there is a big hole in your life? Try following Christ. It does not matter how old you are, what race you are, what gender you are, we are all children of God and He wants us all to walk with Him. Its simple and easy to do. If you don't know Him as your Lord and Savior and you feel you need a change in your life then do what I did, GET IN THE WATER.

Swim around a little and do it faithfully with 100% commitment. If this is what you want then please pray with me these words:

Dear heavenly father, I know I am a sinner, and I ask for Your forgiveness. I believe You died for my sins and You rose from the grave three days later. I want You to come into my life so I can follow You as my Lord and Savior. From this day forward please guide me down the right path so I may do your will. In Your Name I pray. Amen.

If you prayed this prayer and truly believe Jesus Christ is your Lord and Savior and you believe He died on the cross for your sins then welcome to the family of God. Your next step is to get plugged in. Find a good church and get involved, get connected. Start by getting a new bible, there are several to chose from and different types of translations you can get. Mine is the New International Version. I use this one because my pastor preaches from this version on Sunday so its easier for me to follow him when he is reading Gods word. Step out of your comfort zone. Go sing in the choir. Don't be afraid. Being a new child of God is a different experience and it can be difficult at times to do what God wants us to. Imagine driving across the country lets say from Georgia to Washington state. You are enjoying your drive and suddenly you are going up a steep hill, it seems like you will never reach the top. Your car begins to slow down and you are running out of gas, then all of a sudden you make it to the top and you find it to be miraculous. Now you are there for awhile and then all of a sudden down the hill you go dropping like a lead balloon. Now you are in the valley. Discouraging isn't it? My advice is to keep driving, eventually you will start to go back up the mountain and guess what, you will reach the top again. Sometimes you may be in the mid-west where its flat and not much scenery and everything looks the same but then you are back on the mountain top. This will be your experience the rest of your life. Mountains, flatland's and valleys. You can try and fill in the valleys by yourself but its like dodging raindrops, it doesn't work. So here is what you do. Trust God. He is the rock you can stand on. He is a firm foundation, He is steady and does not falter. He is with you always and forever. Stay focused on Him. God knows that we struggle from time to time, and we struggle with finding and hanging onto hope. I know because I have been there. The world these days is filled with insecurities and we even feel uneasy at times. God gives us confidence through His word that He will take care of us. My advice is........**Just keep driving!**

James 1:12 Blessed is the one who perseveres under trial because, having stood the test, that person will receive the crown of life that the Lord has promised to those who love Him.

Mary's story

Proverbs 3:5-6 Trust in the Lord with all your heart and lean not on your own understanding; in all your ways submit to Him, and He will make your path straight.

When I talk about trusting God and following His will it can sometimes be confusing and even uncomfortable. Sometimes it can be very emotional and difficult to understand. We often wonder why bad things happen to good people and why God would allow these things to happen. Our job as Christians is to follow Gods will, to be obedient to what His desires are and to not question what Gods has in store for us. God has a plan, we don't know what it is and we have to accept the fact that He does and will guide us through the troubles we will sometimes face. Its easy for someone to say these things especially when they have not faced a difficult challenge. Mary and I on the other hand did face a difficult challenge, but from from the beginning we trusted God Completely. In September 2019 Mary had a mammogram done and was asked to come back in for another one. The doctor had spotted something on the first one and wanted another look. We began to speculate as to why they wanted another look. We decided to trust God with this circumstance and wait for this outcome. She went back in and had another mammogram done. While she was there they decided she needed to have an ultrasound done. Afterwards Mary was told they would need to do a biopsy of an area they had found on the ultrasound. She called me and told me what was going on and naturally we began to speculate, saying that they just wanted to rule out a problem they had seen. We prayed about it and said we were going to trust that God would take care of this issue in our lives, or should I say in Mary's life. The doctors office had scheduled her biopsy for September 11th but it was later changed to an earlier date of September 3rd. The next day Mary received a phone call advising her that there were two areas they were looking at one was found to be negative but the other was positive for cancer. I had just come home from work when she hung up the phone. It was traumatic news, we both cried with worry. We had known others who had gone through similar situations but never did we think it would be us. We prayed God would take this burden from her. We asked God to take away the worry and to heal Mary either by a miracle or by the doctors hands. We prayed for this to be done quickly but we know that God works in His own timing. We felt at that moment that He had control of everything. I could hear God say "**I GOT THIS**". Mary was having an elective procedure done and was actually scheduled to have it done on the 23rd but that was put on hold until this issue was resolved. Mary called her doctor and told them what was happening and they were able to get her in to see the surgeon that Friday the 6th. We had spoke to three doctors that day, the breast surgeon, medical oncologist and the radiologist. First we spoke to the surgeon. He told us he has a team of doctors that get together twice a month to discuss cases. He was able to assembled his team of doctors and reviewed Mary's case that morning. They already had the pathology reports and he was able to tell us what the plan of attack was going to be. Keep in mind we are only in day three. The outlook was really good and he was wanting to move quickly so we could put this behind us. The medical oncologist actually said it was "divine intervention" because of the way things were moving so quickly. I really liked Gods confirmation there. The next two weeks was brutal for Mary. She had appointments almost every day, MRI, plastic surgeon, genealogist, and cardiologist just to name a few. By weeks end she was exhausted. On Tuesday the 17th we met with the surgeon for another consult. The MRI showed no other issues and we were now ready to schedule Mary for her surgery. She had to meet with the cardiologist one more time before her surgery but a tentative date of October 9th was scheduled. The Genealogist office called and advised Mary she did not have either one of the Brca gene mutations which is good because it would have drastically changed the course of action regarding her surgery. Mary is all done now with all of her appointments and is now waiting to speak with the surgeon again before her surgery. As a husband and now a caregiver I understand now what its like to see someone who is your soulmate and best friend go through this terrible ordeal. I want to take her into my workshop and fix her but I knew I couldn't do that. To see her this way hurts because I'm supposed to protect her. My mistake is thinking that I can fix her. I can't but God can. I have found the best way to help her is to trust

God and to be with her every step of the way. Listening is always best. Mary would vent some times and with me being there to hear her vent made her feel better. To hold her hand or hug her when she needs it or to just pray with her. As I watch Mary during all of this I wonder how she could be so brave. I'm not sure I could be as brave as she is. Her strength is so strong, she knows God is with her and her willingness to follow Gods Will for her is unwavering. I pray for Mary but I also pray for the doctors in her life. I ask for Gods guidance and assurance that all things concerning this issue will be in His hands not ours. I want whoever reads this who may be experiencing the same things may gain strength form Mary and trust God will take care of them too.

2 Samuel 7:28 Sovereign LORD, you are God! Your covenant is trustworthy, and you have promised these good things to your servant.

I am sure Mary feels sometimes these long days will never end, but with Gods assurance we are confident it will end and Gods Will for us will be done. We both know Gods Will in this moment is for us to trust Him and follow the path He has chosen for us. The path is a rocky one right now but with Gods Grace and Mercy it will turn smooth as glass and all the Praise and glory will be given to Him now and forever.

Mary had a follow up appointment with her Pulmonologist on the Wednesday before her surgery and when he found she was having surgery to remove her cancer he was concerned about an area he had seen on her cat scan from an earlier appointment. He now wanted to do a biopsy on that area before she had her surgery. WOW, now we are waiting again. Waiting is the hardest part. Two weeks would go by before we found out the pathology report showed negative. God is so good!

The devil likes to throw his two cents worth in any chance he can and especially during times like this. He knows that if we start to have doubts then he wins. His main goal is to steer us away from our belief if only for a moment so he could get his little piece of victory. Mary and I knew he was just trying to cast doubts in our minds that God will take care of us. Our faith that God is in control did not waiver and God received the victory. What a mighty and powerful God we serve!

Isaiah 26:3 You will keep in perfect peace those whose minds are steadfast, because they trust in you.

Mary's surgery is now back on for Friday October 25, 2019. Mary's surgery went very well, her doctors were confident they got all of the cancer and clear margins around the area were present. Great News! Now comes the after surgery treatment. We knew that radiation treatment was going to happen but we were not sure if chemo was in her future and we had to wait for the lymph nodes to come back from pathology. A week later the pathology report came back negative for any cancer. Mary and I were elated about the news and we just Praised God for the good news. The doctor advised us that all areas surrounding the cancer were clear and no cancer was found through out her body. CANCER FREE! Mary has to do four rounds of chemotherapy and some radiation treatments and she will be done. Hallelujah God is so good.

Jeremiah 30:17 "But I will restore you to health and heal your wounds, declares the Lord"

Mary completed all of her treatments and things went very well. Now she is healing and not from just the physical aspect but also from the mental aspect as well. It does play a toll on the mind. Mary asked if she could put her thoughts on paper and put it in this book. I agreed it would be good for others to read about what she experienced from this challenge. Here is Mary's letter.

Marys letter

Cancer.....This one word brings up terrible thoughts and feelings for so many people. When I heard that word describing what was wrong with me, all I could do was cry. Afraid, and thinking my life would be finishing at age 68, no more time with my wonderful husband and no more time to see my children continue to grow into the strong, self-sufficient young adults they have become. So much going through my head at the same time, and then in a few minutes I was able to really grasp what the doctor was saying. "It's small, we caught it early and you should be just fine."

That was the last week in August, 2019. Between then and now (May, 2020), I have had a lumpectomy, four (4) rounds of chemotherapy and sixteen (16) rounds of radiation. I am waiting to go to the doctor for him to reiterate I am cancer-free.

During this time, I have had many strong feelings about what was happening to me and my body. The anger at first, then the shame, depression and finally now I am accepting this as the new normal for me. I am a cancer survivor and very proud of my status. So many have lost their fight, or have gone through much more than I did. I have made several new friends as we collectively fought cancer together. New friends are always something to be happy about.

This fight began with a prayer from Bob asking for patience and guidance as we traveled this new road. As we walked though this journey, God was with us every step of the way. He showed me that spending time with Bob was very important, spending time with friends was important also. So many times we get caught up in what is going on around us when we need to concentrate on what is happening with us right now. I have realized what is important and it is love, God's love. Love for family and friends, love for the beautiful sky and green trees. All the things God has blessed us with is whats important. We need to all be more thankful of the blessings and gifts that are "free for the taking". I never spent time looking at trees and leaves until now. I would look at the trees on my way to work (3 miles) and try and figure out how many colors of green I saw. I never did figure it out. Too many to count. A beautiful blue sky with wisps of clouds hanging in the air. I am not a big outside person, and have missed so much by being indoors. As campers we spend a lot of time outside at the various campgrounds we visit. Hopefully, I plan to work at being outside more enjoying the breeze, sky and all that God has blessed us with.

Back to the cancer. The biopsy was scheduled in four days, the doctor visits were two days later. I had a couple of other tests which needed to be run, and they were scheduled rather quickly. My surgery was the end of October and then my recuperation began. Chemotherapy started shortly afterwards. I had a special christian friend, Cheryl, who took me to each of my chemo treatments. She was such a positive person and gave me such a safe, secure feeling as we drove to each session. She was unable to take me to my last treatment and so another dear friend took me. She was also named Cheryl. Both Cheryl's are very special to me.

My world is a little different now. So many people traveled this road with Bob and me. There are so many people I must say thank you to. Way too many names to list here. God has blessed Bob and me with many friends from many walks of life. Our families have been so supportive, our friends at church, both our work locations have been there and prayed each day for us. Our camping friends and all the other people that we have known. I had a 50th class reunion last year, and the wife of one of my classmates had been down this road and she spent time with me at the reunion praying especially for me.

I have decided that God can fight my battles now, He is so good at doing that for each of us. All we must do is give it to Him and He will take care of us. His love is all-encompassing, uplifting, forgiving, and breath-taking. Take His hand and follow Him. Life is so much better when you know you are not alone. This is my purpose God has given me and I am running full steam ahead. To God be the Glory.

Philippians 4:13 I can do all this through Him who gives me strength

New challenges are not easy

Even the strongest of Christians find it challenging sometimes. Every one needs to be reminded that Jesus is our Hope and it is offered to us every single day of our lives. My suggestion is to ask a bunch of questions and read your bible. Find a Sunday school class. It is a great place to start. You will be surprised with the people you will meet who have the same beliefs and struggles as you. Your spiritual journey has begun. You must now learn how to communicate with God, how to understand and listen to what God wants with us, and how to start a life centered around your commitment to Him. There are books out there you can get to help you study your bible, devotionals to help with your time in the scriptures and with the

Lord. When I became a christian I found this bible verse to help me when I would get discouraged. I still depend on it today.

Joshua 1:9 Have I not commanded you? Be strong and courageous. Do not be afraid; do not be discouraged, for the Lord your God will be with you where ever you go.

Find your bible verse and hold onto it tight. Be patient and stay strong in your faith. Give God your best effort. God gave His all so you should too. Don't settle for minimal things or set small goals. God is bigger than anything you can dream up and He will always walk with you through it all. Satan wins when you can give more and don't. When you surrender to His will then you will accomplish everything He has in store for you. Praise Him for the good and the bad. If you prayed for that new job you were completely qualified for and didn't get it then praise Him for closing the door. It was probably not in His will for you to have it. I was offered a job and I was not even looking for one. I took it and it has been a blessing. What ever God calls you to be or do then believe me God will provide everything you will need to succeed. Gods Grace and mercy has stood the test of time so trust in Him completely. You will not regret it, I promise!

Oh where oh where is my purpose? Okay.... here it is!

Being at the high school was very rewarding for me. God had me there for a reason and I tried my best to do His will. Working with the kids was a blessing in so many ways. Some may not think so but I do. I often wondered why He had me there. There were highs and lows, good and bad, sad and happy, successes and failures, tragedies and triumphs but through it all God was there. Have I found my purpose? **So..I wanted to see my purpose.....here it is.** God has shown me it has never been about __my purpose__ its has always been about __His Purpose__. Purpose to believe, to trust, to love, to endure, to forgive, to pray, to listen, to praise, to reject sin, to accept, to sing, to fulfill, to follow, to lead, to be faithful, to ask and so many more things. My purpose is to follow Gods will whatever that may be. I must listen to Him and do what is commanded of me. My purpose is to follow His Purpose. Gods word offers so many insights to this. We all have a purpose in life. God has us all on different mission fields for Him. I would not even try to figure out who has what or when. I know now God wants me to follow His will and that's what I am going to do. We need to hear what God is telling us. Learning to listen to God can be difficult at times and I for one believe we need to stop talking and start listening. Even the slightest things could be God telling you what He wants from you. Learn to pay attention.

Final Thought.....almost!

So here we are, nearing the end of this book. I have never seen myself as a good writer but I hope this was a good read for you. These words have come from my heart and I hope they have encouraged you into at least thinking about changing your life. To accept Jesus Christ as your Lord and Savior. As a former Police Officer things can get pretty hectic at times and in some cases you could be responding to a serious call where you are thinking this may be the time you don't go home. You start thinking about what if I don't go home will my family be taken care of. You think about the call and how you are going to handle it and then you trust your training to help you through it. I also had God on my side. He gave me comfort in knowing He would take care of me. There was comfort in knowing He would take care of my family. Every experience I have had with Christ has been a blessing in one form or another. When you read through these words I wanted to make sure it is about forgiveness and purpose. I have seen and done both. If Lonna and I did not know Christ I firmly believe we would not have been able to forgive each other. We are good friends today and I value our friendship. We never saw the world as a big place until we got in it. I don't regret any of my life and I thank God for all of it. I have had some experiences that I can now share so others don't make the same mistakes I did. Sometimes we have to fall pretty hard to finally see the truth. I did not go all the way to the bottom of the barrel but I can say it was in reach. I am six foot three and at one point I weighted 145 pounds. I can tell you drinking instead of eating does not help, it only makes matters worse. My life was in shambles from the start and I had nobody to blame but myself. From troubles at birth, to being a rebellious teen, not having a stable job, two failed marriages, separation from my children, and an abusive boss to mention a few.

Some of these things I could control and others I could not but now I know the truth. God is faithful to those who believe and as for me, I believe. The drinking, smoking, cursing and looking for another failed marriage all stopped. Why? Because I gave it all to Christ. He took it all away. He was with me and guided me every step of the way. I am now able to walk with God and do His work with confidence and assurance. If you look at all the things I lost before I knew Christ and then look at the things I have gained since I found Christ, then its a No-brainer. I tried to fix it all by myself and look how that turned out. Now He has given me a Job which I kept for 28 years and retired from. He gave me a beautiful wife who I adore and love very much, we love and trust each other completely. She has been by my side through it all, holding my hand and wiping my tears. What an amazing woman. We have a great church to go to every Sunday where I sing in the choir. I sometimes have tears falling down my face because I know Jesus paid and gave it all. If I was the only one on planet earth who needed saving, Christ would have still died on that old rugged cross. I was able to meet with a daughter who I did not know even existed. What a blessing that journey has been. I even have a new granddaughter as well. We meet from time to time and enjoy each others company. I hope maybe one day that relationship will get closer but I'm Okay with the way things are now. I struggle sometimes to follow Him but I know He is with me. I have never looked back. I often wonder how I even deserve the gifts and blessing God has given me. He has blessed me beyond measure and has done things for me I could never repay. God only wants our total devotion to Him like He has given us. So as for me and my house we will serve the Lord.

A LETTER FROM LONNA

When God allows Forgiveness

I grew up in southern New Hampshire. I have a brother close in age and a sister who is 12 years younger. My father and mother divorced when I was twelve. After the divorce things were difficult for my mother trying to raise three children on her own. She must have cried behind closed doors because she never showed how much she was struggling. At 14, I met Bob who happened to be a friend of my brother. Bob and his family lived in the same town as my family. Laughs and giggles turned into dating. My mother never objected to the dating despite Bob being four years older. My grades started to fail and I was hanging out a lot with Bob and our friends. I was feeling so in love!

Bob joined the Air Force and I was heart broken. I missed him terribly. I really can't recall when marriage came up, but I think the plan was to join the Air Force then we could marry. We were married in a catholic church in our home town. I really didn't know much about God and at the time it really wasn't an interest. At the young age of sixteen my mother and I were planning my wedding. When I look back I can't fathom my mother allowing this. I know she liked Bob and maybe she thought this would be good as she was struggling.

I turned seventeen and ten days later I was married and on my way to Texas. After the first few weeks I really started to miss home. I also realized I knew nothing about marriage and what it stood for. I can't speak for Bob but I think we were just so immature. We really had no guidance and direction. We really didn't have a plan. We just knew Bob had a job and we were together. I was with the person I loved. We were still having parties as if living a college dorm life. I was so young and immature I didn't even know how to cook spaghetti, nor did I know how to grocery shop or do a budget. I knew nothing but hanging with friends who were always much older than me. We had lots of parties, Bob and I never spoke of God or even thought to seek out a church.

Things eventually calmed down when I became pregnant. Pregnant at eighteen and a newborn at nineteen. This was not a planned pregnancy. We never sat down and talked about starting a family. I was so scared. I remember sitting on the edge of my bed at night crying about being a mother. I had no family with me but I had one girlfriend who turned out to be a huge role model for me. I learned everything from her. I grew up a lot in the years we were together. We are still best friends today.

We were always struggling with not having any money. Military pay is hard enough to live on and we were being so foolish with our money. We were always behind on something. God still wasn't a thought for us.

Shortly after Sheila was born we moved into base housing. I was pregnant again and had our second child. It was only about three months later we were moving to Lakenheath England. There was a lot of excitement with going to a foreign country and it didn't take long for me to become bored. I felt very much alone. Because of my immaturity I was mad at my husband for having me in this situation! The partying started again with military members who lived in the same housing as us and I started to really struggle. I was not easy to please. I don't think I even knew what I wanted. I felt isolated, alone and stuck with two small children. I was missing home more and more and I ended up going back to the states. Still neither one of us considering God.

While back in the states I found myself doing the party scene again. I liked being with my friends. I found a small job which was short lived. During this time I met an older guy and I ended up having a relationship with him for a couple of months. I'm not sure how it came up with me going back to England but I found my way back. I thought things were good and at one point I got into a dental assisting program and I was working now. I came back to the states with Bob when he received orders to Mississippi. I stayed with my mom until base housing came up. I was actually excited about going. I had some work experience and a more positive outlook for our family.

Now in Mississippi I became miserable. I wanted to work but there was nothing in the Dental field which is what I wanted to do after my training in England. Eventually I found a job at a fast food restaurant. I started making friends and the partying started again.

Our marriage was becoming strained again. I really can't blame much on Bob. I put a lot of pressure on him. I actually was horrible to him when I look back at it. We still did not know God. We were not doing anything as a couple either and that probably had a lot to do with me. Bob was always working hard and nothing was ever good enough for me. I ended up becoming friends with the person I am married to now. He was working evenings at the fast food restaurant where I was working. Eventually it turned into an affair. At this point there was no saving our marriage. I was flooded with so many promises of how good life was going to be. I thought I found everything I had been lacking, the truth is, I was never lacking anything. I had myself in quite a mess. I was confused with the pull from my boyfriend and the thought of really leaving Bob. I will never forget the last good bye with my husband, I can play it in my head to this day. Saying good bye was the worst decision of my life! I don't know where or how we would have ended up if we once again tried to make it work. I was such a lost soul. We still had no clue about God. Bob and I didn't talk much after our divorce unless I was harassing him for more child support. There came a time when our two girls had to spend some time with Bob so I could get my feet on the ground and into an apartment. I believe we became cordial towards each other during this time. Eventually the girls came back with me. At some point my husband starting talking to me about Christ. I was very interested and we started attending Merrimack Valley Baptist. I accepted the Lord as my Savior and became a member of the church.

Much time has passed now. The girls had graduated and moved on. Our youngest daughter Julia joined the Navy. She became pregnant and gave birth to our first granddaughter. We were not expecting to be grandparents and we didn't even know she was pregnant, but it happened and we are now grandparents. My oldest daughter Sheila and I traveled to Florida to be with Julia. Bob and his wife Mary traveled down to visit with Julia and his granddaughter as well. There was a bit of uneasiness because this was going to be the first time we were going to see each other in many years. I truly had a sense of peace with me. I had God! It was strangely exciting to see Bob and meet his wife Mary. There was peace in the air. I was happy they were there. Something was taking place in the room with us. There was a lot of talking and crying! We started praying and asking each other for forgiveness, asking God for His forgiveness. It felt like there was a huge cleansing of my soul. In Gods rightful time He had allowed forgiveness. God forgave me of my sins and It was a beautiful moment.

It took many years for Bob and I to finally forgive each other and to put our differences aside. Neither one of us are blaming each other now and there is no more arguing about petty issues. Our girls were extremely happy when we finally allowed this to happen. They were able to talk more openly with us about their issues. They liked it now that we are no longer arguing. God has transformed a bad situation into something amazing and beautiful. Before Bob and I were married we were really good friends and now we are again. We laugh at the old times and we even talk about the bad times and how silly we were acting. Only God can do the things that has been done and all of the Praise goes to Him. Our girls have given us five amazing grandchildren and its only through Gods grace that we are able to visit with them together without feeling uncomfortable or being fake with our emotions when we are together or having to visit them separately because we cant be around each other. Life is way too short for this type of foolishness to continue. My prayers were answered and forgiveness was given. I may have even found my purpose.

2 Corinthians 5:18 All this is from God, who reconciled us to Himself through Christ and gave us the ministry of reconciliation

Final thought for sure!

I have a bucket list....you know....a list where you write things down that you want to do before you "kick the bucket" and as you do the things on your list you cross them out. Well the first thing on my list is to Honor and Glorify our Lord and Savior Jesus Christ. My prayer is when I get to heaven Jesus will be standing there with my list in His hands smiling, then takes His mighty pen and crosses out those words at the top of my list. Now I get to praise and worship Him forever in heaven. What a mighty and wonderful God we serve. For the last 30 years I have been serving Him and I will never, as Luke Skywalker said "I'll never turn to the DARK SIDE"! That's for all you Star Wars people.

Hebrews 13:5 Never will I leave you; never will I forsake you.

FINAL PRAYER

THANK YOU JESUS FOR MY NEW LIFE. FOR SHOWING ME YOUR PURPOSE, FOR GIVING ME THE STRENGTH TO FORGIVE AND TO LOVE AGAIN. THANK YOU FOR EVERYONE WHO READS THESE WORDS AND FINDS YOU AS THEIR LORD AND SAVIOR. MAY ALL THE HONOR AND GLORY AND PRAISE BE GIVEN TO YOU FOR EVERYTHING YOU HAVE DONE AND WILL DO FOR US. I PRAY THAT YOU WILL HELP ME WHEN I AM WEAK AND WHEN I AM IN THE MIDST OF THE CHAOS OF THE WORLD. I PRAY THAT I WILL HAVE THE STRENGTH TO LAY AT YOUR FEET ALL OF THE TRIALS THAT I WILL FACE IN THE FUTURE AND NOT TO DEPEND ON MYSELF

ALONE. I PRAY THAT I KEEP MY EYES ON YOU AND TO CONTINUE TO LIVE MY LIFE AS YOU WOULD WANT ME TOO. THANK YOU FOR LOVING ME WHEN I DID NOT DESERVE IT. THANK YOU FOR THE CROSS AND YOUR SACRIFICE.   IN JESUS NAME.

AMEN

Last word

Romans 8:38-39

For I am convinced that neither death nor life,

neither angels nor demon, neither the present

nor the future, nor any powers, neither height

nor depth, nor anything else in all creation,

will be able to separate us from the love of God

that is in Christ Jesus our Lord.

Paul the Apostle

Made in the USA
Columbia, SC
15 May 2020